HORRIBLE HISTORIES

P9-CRT-726

BARMY
BRITISH EMPIRE

Terry Deary Illustrated by Martin Brown

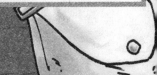

SCHOLASTIC

For Ronan Paterson – a star.

Scholastic Children's Books,
Euston House, 24 Eversholt Street,
London NW1 1DB, UK

A division of Scholastic Ltd
London ~ New York ~ Toronto ~ Sydney ~ Auckland
Mexico City ~ New Delhi ~ Hong Kong

First published in the UK by Scholastic Ltd, 2002
This edition published 2017

Text © Terry Deary, 2002
Illustrations © Martin Brown, 2002
All rights reserved

ISBN 978 1407 16700 8

Printed and bound by CPI Group (UK) Ltd, Croydon, CR0 4YY

6 8 10 9 7

www.scholastic.co.uk

CONTENTS

Introduction 5

Terrible timeline 7

Early Empire 11

Savage slavers 20

Incredible India 42

Empress's quick eastern quiz 46

Dreadful down under 53

Awful for animals 66

Gruesome games and sick sports 74

Heroes of the British Empire 80

Nasty natives 95

Epilogue 125

Grisly Quiz 129

Interesting Index 137

Introduction

What's an empire? It's a collection of countries all ruled by one emperor. You know the sort of thing – you start with one greedy little state like Rome and, before you know it, you have a Roman Empire. Everyone ruled by a super Caesar like the nutty Nero or the horrible Hadrian.

Sounds cosy, doesn't it? Well, it's not really because most of the time those countries don't *want* to be ruled by the emperor! He just sent his bully-boys in to take it over.

Imagine what that must be like! You've lived in your house all your life and enjoyed it. You're sitting at home one day when in marches a bunch of soldiers and they say…

And that's how it was with the British Empire till about 1900. The Brits just marched into somebody's country and said, 'We're in charge!' And it got worse…

Of course, it was never quite so simple. People rebelled against the British – some succeeded and some failed. Either way, lots of people died … horribly. In fact the history of the British Empire is full of horrible people and horrible deeds. Just the sort of stuff for a Horrible History.

And, as it happens, you're reading one now! Read on…

Terrible Timeline

Every day, somewhere in the British Empire, someone suffered. Here are just a few of the highlights – or, if you were a victim, the lowlights – of the empire up till 1900...

1562 England begins its slave trade thanks to her Terrible Tudor superior sailors. They buy people in Africa and sell them to South America.

1607 The British start to settle in America. They push the Indians out of the way and start to grow tobacco and cotton and sugar (in the West Indies). But this is hard work and the Brits don't like it! So they need even more slaves to do the work for them.

1619 The first slaves arrive in North America and the West Indies from Africa. Sugar is popular and a huge number of slaves are sent to America to grow sugar cane.

1620 The 'Pilgrim Fathers' land on the north-east coast of America and set up a colony. They will cause trouble later.

1652 The Dutch set up a colony of 'Boers' (or farmers) in South Africa. They'll cause trouble later too!

1756–63 The Seven Years War against France and Spain. The Brits win and become the main rulers of India's incredible riches through the East India Company – a powerful trading company, backed by the British Army.

1770 Captain Cook comes across Australia. A whacking great chunk of land to add to the empire. Loads of empty space to dump convicts (from 1788). Shame the Brits taught them to play cricket.

1770 British explorer James Bruce reaches the source of the Blue Nile.

1776 The American settlers rebel against their British rulers. The Brits lose their big rich American colony so it's time to set off to take over the rest of the world! Look out world!

1789 Freed slave Olaudah Equiano publishes his life story. This helps the growing 'Abolitionist' struggle in Britain and the US to banish all slavery.

1792 There is a slave rebellion in Haiti led by Toussant L'Ouverture (1743-1803). His army of 55,000 blacks fights against the French and makes them think slavery is not such a good idea.

1795 The Brits take over the Cape Colony (South Africa) from the

Dutch – known as 'Boers' – which is a bit of a boering name. The Boers begin to move inland in search of better land and to escape British control. Those Boers will be a nuisance for the next hundred years or more.

1818 Shaka, the Zulu chief, launches the Mfecane (Wars Of Crushing And Wandering) against his black African neighbours and the white Europeans in southern Africa.

1834 Slavery is abolished in the British Empire … sort of! The slaves have to stay with their masters for four more years.

1838 768,000 slaves free at last. But many native lords in Empire countries keep slaves and the Brits can't do anything about it.

1839 The First Opium War – the Brits fight for the right to sell opium to the Chinese. Opium is making Brit drug dealers very rich … and the Chinese very dead.

1851 Gold is discovered in Australia. Hope those convicts don't pinch it!

1855 Scottish missionary David Livingstone explores the Zambezi River in Africa and names the Victoria Falls after his queen. (What a creep!)

1857 The Indian Mutiny. The Brits are shocked to find that the Indians do NOT like the Brits! Vicious fighting and cruelty on both sides.

1860 The Maori Wars in New Zealand. As usual the war ends in gore.

1876 Queen Victoria is crowned Empress of India. No one has asked the Indians, of course.

1879 The Zulu War. William Gladstone says: 'Ten thousand Zulus died and their only crime was to try and defend their families against the British guns.'

1899 The Second Boer War. The mighty Brit Empire struggles to beat a few farmers. It's the beginning of the end for the Empire.

Early Empire

By the 1600s British people had set out and begun to settle in America. Some were looking for freedom – they were Puritan Christians who were having a hard time at home.

When they arrived in America they found there were people already there – Native Americans. But the Christians didn't mind! The Christians believed their God had *planned* it that way! In 1625 Simon Purchas, a churchman, said…

God is wise and he made these savage countries rich so the riches will be attractive to Christians!

Kind person, the Christian God! Can you really imagine him saying . . .

LOOK, LADS, I MADE A RICH LAND AND FILLED IT WITH NATIVES. THE NATIVES DIDN'T DO A VERY GOOD JOB OF LOOKING AFTER IT. SO I'M SENDING YOU CHRISTIANS TO SHOW THEM THE WAY! THE RICHES ARE YOUR REWARD

The Christians really *believed* this. They also believed they were *better* than the Indians because they used tablecloths and the Indians didn't! Honest! In 1580 Brit explorer Martin

Frobisher came across the Inuit (Eskimos) in Canada and said…

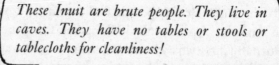

These Inuit are brute people. They live in caves. They have no tables or stools or tablecloths for cleanliness!

Er, hang on, Mr Frobisher … if they have no *tables* then *of course* they have no tablecloths! And are you saying people who don't use tablecloths are brutes? Well, there are an awful lot of children who eat school dinners without tablecloths! Are they all brutes?

YOU REALLY WANT ME TO ANSWER THAT?

At first the Indians were friendly, so the Brit invaders decided to teach them how to be good Christians – with tablecloths. But when fighting broke out the Brits decided the Indians wouldn't make good Christians after all. Instead they treated the Indians like wild animals – to be hunted and killed. A 1622 book of rules for Brit tobacco planters in Virginia said…

It is easier to conquer the Indians than to teach them. For they are simple, naked people, scattered in small villages and this makes them easy to defeat. In future it will be our job to make them obey by destroying their villages and crops. They can then be chased on our horses, tracked by bloodhounds and torn to pieces with our mastiff dogs for these people are no better than wild beasts.

For the next 300 years the Brits treated everyone else the same way – in Africa, Australia, New Zealand and Ireland for example. The rules were:

British settlers remember

1 Natives are simple people

2 It is our job to teach them how to be British and Christian

3 If they rebel then they will have to be destroyed

It was nonsense, but the Brits BELIEVED it. Sadly some British people in the twenty-first century *still* believe that they are better than others!

Better Brits

The Brits believed they were 'better' than the native peoples in many ways:

1 In seventeenth-century America, Brit invaders looked at the Indians with disgust because they wandered around with hardly any clothes on. But the Barmy Brits wore *too many* clothes. The ones who laughed at naked Indians were wearing hot and heavy white wigs. And in steaming eighteenth-century India, soldiers wore red woollen tunics buttoned up to the neck and felt hats. The officers wore white gloves too! One group of soldiers arrived in India wearing brass helmets under a fierce sun – this 'cooked' their heads and many died from sunstroke. And you thought school uniform was bad!

2 Over in Ireland in 1823 the Brits sneered at the 9,000 Irish people of Tullahobagly for being so poor. These 9,000 Irish had just 93 chairs between them and only 10 beds. But the Brit capital of London was no better. There was terrible poverty and the streets were full of beggars. In fact, there were so many that some of them had to cheat to get people's attention. They would…

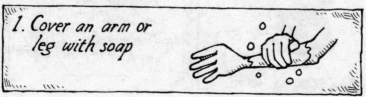

1. Cover an arm or leg with soap

2. Soak the soapy arm in vinegar until it bubbles and blisters

3. The arm now looks as if it has been scalded

OW! OW!

4. Go out on the street and beg for money

ALMS! ALMS! I'VE BURNT ME ARMS

3 The Brits believed they were braver than foreign soldiers – even the foreign soldiers who fought with the British army. In 1883 Valentine Baker led a force of a few Brits and a few thousand Egyptians against the Dervishes of Sudan. The Brits and Egyptians had machine guns – the Dervishes had wooden clubs and knives. Baker said the Brits showed courage while the Egyptians panicked – the Egyptians fell to their knees and begged for their lives as their throats were cut. Of course the Brits (Baker said) fought bravely on ... with machine guns against clubs, of course!

Making masses of money

Money, money, money. That's what the British Empire was built on. And where there's money there's greed and there's trouble. At least those Christian settlers got one thing right...

15

The British Empire builders certainly did love money a lot – so, of course, they created a lot of evil.

Those early Christians didn't leave Britain just to find natives and turn them into Christians. They left Britain to make their fortunes. How did they do that? Through 'trade'. Here's how to do it...

You can see why the British set out to find as many countries as they could to trade with. They could get tea from India, sheep from Australia and New Zealand, gold and diamonds from Africa. But a new trade grew that made even more money! The slave trade! Here's how it worked...

4. UNLOAD THE SHIP AND SWAP THE GOODS FOR THINGS THAT THEY ARE SHORT OF IN AMERICA–SLAVES
SO FAR SO GOOD!
5. SAIL TO AMERICA
IT'S A GOOD LIFE!
IF YOU'RE NOT A SLAVE!
6. SWAP THE SLAVES FOR SUGAR, COTTON, TOBACCO AND RUM, THEN SAIL BACK TO BRITAIN AND SELL THEM FOR FAR MORE THAN YOU PAID FOR THE BRITISH LOAD
GOOD IDEA THIS TRADING GAME!

Savage slavers

Find that slave

Where did slaves come from? Mostly from Africa where African slave traders sold other Africans to the Brits. But where did *they* go to get a slave? After all, they couldn't just pop down to the local supermarket, pick up a few and flog them to the British slavers. Slave dealers in Africa either got them from tribes who had captured prisoners from other tribes in war or they simply kidnapped them.

Olaudah Equiano was captured when he was a child and sold as a slave. He is one of the few slaves who survived to write his own story. Olaudah said…

The grown-ups of our village used to go off to work in the fields. The children then gathered together to play. But whenever we played we always sent someone up a tree to watch out for the slave dealers. This was the time when slave dealers rushed into the village, snatched as many children as they could, and carried them off to the coast. There they were sold as slaves.

Imagine that! You go to play in your local park and before you know it a gang has picked you up and sold you! You'd never see your home or your family again. Cruel.

Some slave dealers even got slaves from tribes who no longer wanted them in their tribe! A tribe might sell a criminal as a slave – which is a bit like your school selling you because you let down the head teacher's car tyres. (Actually, you probably deserve it!) But they also sold people who broke the rules of the tribe. One of the saddest cases was when they sold a woman whose 'crime' was ... having twins!

Check that slave

Only fit Africans were bought as slaves, and the slaves knew that! So what would *you* do if you were going to be sold? Pretend to be sick?

Sadly this would not work.

Not all slavers picked carefully, though. Some slaves were sent to the ships even though they looked too ill to survive the journey. In 1751 ship's captain John Newton reported…

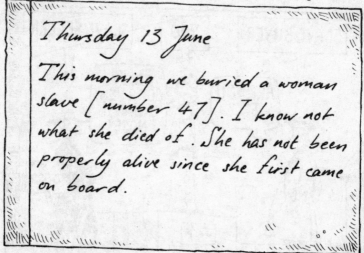

Thursday 13 June

This morning we buried a woman slave [number 47]. I know not what she died of. She has not been properly alive since she first came on board.

So when you died you weren't even buried with your name – just a number.

Bung that slave

Slaves were worth a lot of money but the traders didn't take very good care of them. Many died, packed into dark, stinking rooms below the decks of the ships. The sailors *did* wash them down every day, though probably by throwing a bucket of sea water over them.

A young slave described the journey of between 40 and 70 days across the Atlantic Ocean...

The stench and the heat was dreadful. The crowding meant you hardly had room to turn over. The chains rubbed some Africans raw. The filth was made worse by the lavatory bucket and many small children fell into it. One day two of my countrymen were allowed on deck. They were chained together and decided they would rather have death than such a life of misery. They jumped into the sea.

He explained how...

- the 'holds' on the ship were about 1.52 metres high and slaves were allowed just half a litre of water a day.
- the food was a vegetable mush and the slaves were told exactly how to eat: 'Pick up the food – put it in your mouth – swallow it!' (Sounds like a good idea for school dinners.)

- on long journeys food and fresh water supplies got low and the captain threw weak slaves – alive – into the ocean so the fit would survive.
- slaves who died were usually thrown over the side to feed the fishes while others arrived in America very sick.

But the traders could deal with sick slaves – sometimes in a quite disgusting way. One of the most common diseases was dysentery – which gives you very bad diarrhoea. Not many Americans would buy a slave with poo dribbling down their legs, would they? So what did the slave traders do? They cut a length of rope and stuffed it up the bum of the slave with diarrhoea and blocked it for a while. That way they could fool their customers into a sale.

Did you know...?
While the slaves were eating vegetable mush the slave-traders back in Britain had more food than they knew what to do with. In 1769 slave-trader William Beckford had a feast. Six hundred dishes were served on golden plates. It cost £10,000.

Sell that slave

You've seen New Year sales in shops, haven't you? People queue for hours to get a bargain, the doors open and the people in the queue all rush in because the first in get the best bargains. Some slave sales in the West Indies could be just like that. They were called 'scrambles'. Olaudah Equiano described one…

1

The signal to start the scramble was the beat of a drum.

2

The buyers rushed into the yard where the slaves were caged and chose the ones they liked best.

3

The noise and the bawling, the greed on the faces of the buyers, made the Africans more terrified.

> *That's how families and friends were separated. Most of them never saw one another again.*

Brand that slave

Ever had a new bike? Afraid of having it stolen? Some people have their post code stamped on the bike frame so it can be recognized. Slaves were not much different. But the 'stamp' was a red-hot 'brand' that was burned into their flesh.

A trader, William Bosman, described what happened in 1705...

> *When we buy slaves they are all examined by our doctors. Those who pass the examination are put to one side. Meanwhile our iron brands are heating in the fire. When we have agreed the price, our slaves are marked on the chest.*

Work that slave

Have you ever taken notes while the teacher speaks? Everyone has to work at the same speed – fine if you're a fast writer, but misery if you are slow. Slaves were organized in gangs and worked a bit like that. All together. Fine if you were fit and fast – but torture if you were old, sick or slow. An 'overseer' stood behind you with a whip and lashed you if you fell behind. It wasn't unusual for a slow slave to be whipped to death. (At least your teacher doesn't do that!) And it wasn't much better for children. They had jobs too, perhaps pulling up weeds. Back-breaking, finger-aching, sweat-making, bone-wearying work, all day long – with that whip cracking behind you to keep you at it. (And you thought PE lessons were bad!)

I'M NOT YOUR SPORTS TEACHER, I'M YOUR SPORTS OVERSEER!

Did you know…?
In 1700 Bristol and Liverpool were small fishing ports. Thanks to the slave trade they grew over the next 100 years and some slave-traders became enormously rich. Many of Bristol and Liverpool's fine buildings were built with the profits of slavery. As a Bristol historian put it:

Every brick in the city of Bristol is cemented with the blood of a slave.

Play like a slave
Some slaves tried to cheer themselves up by making music. They often sang songs that made fun of their white masters!

27

They even made their own instruments – drums, whistles, and banjos from wood and string. Here are a couple you may like to try…

Make a shaky-shekie
You need:
A piece of wood.
Two sticks.

To play:
Place the wood across your knees.
Beat the wood with the sticks.

SHACKETY-SHECKETY
SHACKETY-SHECKETY

Make a kitty-kattie
You need:
A dead pig – rip out its belly (or bladder).
A handful of dried peas.

KITTELY-KATTELY

KITTELY-KATTELY

To play:
Push the peas inside the pig's bladder.
Blow up the bladder till it is tight.
Tie the end.
Shake the kitty-kattie like a rattle.

What do you mean? You don't fancy blowing into a pig's belly? Oh, all right. Try it with a balloon instead!

Slave fight-backs

What could you *do* about being a slave? Hell, you could always *die* – of overwork or disease. In 1792 half the slaves on one Jamaica farm died in their first four years there. But if you survived you might have tried for a better life. How?

28

a) Run away

Difficult, because you were often forced to work in chains. And risky, because if you were caught you'd be lashed, or have your ears cut off or be executed. In 1776 in East Jamaica slave 'Jack' escaped. He was caught. The judge gave his decision…

b) Rebel

That doesn't mean you had to punch your owner on his nose. Slaves rebelled in other ways. They could simply make life difficult for their owners…

Slaves often got away with it. The owners thought these things happened because slaves were stupid and clumsy, but it was the owners who were stupid for thinking that!

One slave boy (in St Vincent, the West Indies, in 1820) wasn't worried about *what* the owners thought. He was left in charge of a large supper table while a ladies' group held a meeting. The meeting finished, the ladies arrived in the supper room ... and there was nothing left but the empty dishes!

Ban that slave

Slavery was abolished in the British Empire in 1834 ... but not everyone agreed that that was a good idea. A writer called Boswell said...

Slaves are owned by people. So, taking the slaves away from their owner is robbery!

Of course Mr Boswell *wasn't* a slave, was he? He probably would NOT have wanted to be 'owned' by anyone! The silly man went on...

There have always been slaves because God wanted it that way!

Maybe batty Boswell had had a chat with God and knew what God wanted … but I doubt it. But his craziest claim was…

> *Banning slavery is cruel to the slaves, especially the Africans. Being a slave to the British Empire has given many of them a much happier life!*

HE CANNOT BE SERIOUS

Maybe brain-dead Boswell hadn't read the newspapers at that time. They listed the cruelties slaves suffered in the British West Indies:

Punishments for slaves who do wrong

1 Being nailed to a post by the ear

2. Having ear cut off

3. Having teeth pulled out

4. Having hands cut off

5. Being fastened in tight steel neck-collars

6. Having eyes gouged out

Still think slaves are 'happier', Mr Boswell?

Party time

In Falmouth the Baptist Church celebrated the end of slavery on the night of 31 July 1838. As midnight drew near the Reverend William Knibb cried…

The monster is dying!

Then as the clock struck midnight he shouted…

The monster is dead!

Then they held a funeral for the slavery 'monster'. They buried chains, whips and iron collars in a grave and sang...

*Now slavery we lay thy vile form in the dust
And buried forever let it there remain!
And rotted and covered with villainy's rust
Be every man-whip and fetter and chain.*

Having a funeral service for an evil thing sounds like a good way to celebrate.

HORRIBLE HISTORIES HEALTH WARNING: The Brits abolished slavery and ever since school history books have been patting the Brits on the back for that! The books sometimes 'forget' to mention the millions of miserable slaves that made millions of pounds for brutal Brits in the 200 years before they banned it.

So, slavery was banished (almost) from the British Empire ... but the Empire only grew stronger.

After slavery

What could the British Empire do with all the free slaves? They couldn't return them to the countries where their grandparents and great-grandparents had been kidnapped – there was nothing there for the ex-slaves.

Someone had the bright idea of giving the freed slaves their own country on the coast of West Africa. The Spanish name for that country was Sierra Leone and the capital city was named Freetown … of course.

Did you know…?

The ex-slaves came from all over and they brought their own ways of life with them. Some of them brought some strange superstitions and they especially hated the British redcoat soldiers. So the superstitions about the redcoats were very odd…

Of course this wasn't true. You will NOT pass your school exams by drinking a brew made from the boiled head of your history teacher!

35

Rotten rebels

In Jamaica the slaves were free – free to starve on the pitiful wages they could earn. By 1865 they were desperate and wrote to Queen Victoria for help. The reply (from Queen Vic's ministers, of course) was…

Riots began when a Jamaican boy was arrested for attacking a woman in his village. A mob marched on the town of Stony Gut – a mob of 500 Jamaicans armed with sticks, cutlasses, fishing spears and a few guns. The town guard turned out to face them. But who started the trouble? The women!

The women had marched into town with their baskets full of stones and they began to throw them. When a stone hit the commander of the guard he ordered his men to open fire. The crowd rushed at them and began a murderous massacre…

- One soldier was killed with a harpoon.
- A Councillor, Baron Von Ketelhodt, was hacked to death and his fingers cut off by the rioters as prizes.
- It was said that the rebels cut out the tongue of preacher the Reverend Herschell while he was still alive, then tried to skin him.
- Lieutenant Hall was pushed into a burning building to roast alive.
- A Jamaican priest (but friend of the Brits) was beaten to death and his guts ripped out.

- British Governor Edward Eyre said…

Many are said to have had their eyes scooped out, their heads split open and their brains taken out.

Governor's Eyre's revenge was terrible. Here are some of his vicious punishments…

- One rebel called Wellington was shot and then had his head hacked off. The body was buried by a stream, but heavy rain swelled the stream and washed the head away. It was found and stuck on a pole – a cruel stunt from the Middle Ages.
- At Fonthill village nine men were shot then hung up in their local church – something Henry VIII had done over 300 years before to rebels in England.
- Over 600 were flogged – and the Brits often put strands of wire in the lashes to make them more painful.
- Jamaicans were hunted down and shot or hanged. Some were given trials and some weren't. A thousand homes were burned to the ground and 439 Jamaicans were killed.
- Men were lined up at a trench and shot so their bodies fell into the trench – a method the Nazis used 80 years later. The Nazis were murderers … and so was Governor Eyre. He was sacked, but he escaped real punishment. Many Brits thought he was a hero.

Painful punishments

The British didn't just move into another country and trade with the people. They liked to make sure the native people lived the British way with British law and order. But some British 'justice' was a bit horrible...

The wicked whip.

Slaves had to obey. If they were cheeky or tried to run away they were punished. Usually with the whip. The women were usually stripped naked and held down by fellow slaves while their owner or overseer ordered a black male slave-driver to flog them. An American slave song described the punishment...

O master! O master!
One Monday morning they lay me down,
And give me thirty-nine on my bare rump,
O master, O master!

The 'thirty nine' lashes were usually one for every year of the slave's life. Pity the ones that lived to seventy!

The brutal bastinado

In Beirut the Brit governor, Colonel Hugh Rose, ordered a man to be punished with the 'bastinado'. Would you like this?

The Beirut criminal's two partners got an easier punishment ... they were ordered to sweep the street!

The hideous hanging

In Morant Bay, Jamaica, there was a rebellion of free slaves in 1865. Several British men and women were killed and Governor Edward Eyre decided to teach the rebels a lesson. He wrote…

> *I came up with a plan which struck terror into those wretched men FAR more than death. I made them hang each other! They begged to be shot rather than do this.*

Governor Eyre said gleefully...

> *The effect on the living was terrifying!*

Nasty. There were hundreds hanged this way – including a Jamaican priest, the Reverend G. W. Gordon. MOST of the hanged men were probably innocent!

Foul fire

In 1760 there was a West Indies slave rebellion known as 'Tacky's Revolt'. One rebel was caught and executed by 'slow burning':

- He was chained to an iron post.
- A fire was lit under his feet.
- He watched as his legs were turned to ashes.

It's said that the rebel suffered this bravely and did not cry out or even groan.

The blasting barrel

In 1832, in India, some Muslims were afraid the British would force them to become Christians. Four Muslims plotted to massacre some Europeans in Bangalore. Their plot was discovered and their punishment was horribly messy…

- The four men were led to the place of execution by a band playing the 'Dead March'.
- They were tied to cannon barrels.
- The cannon were fired … and the men blown to little pieces.

The sweet treatment

In 1756, in Jamaica, a starving slave was caught eating the sugar cane he was supposed to be collecting. The slave owner's diary reported…

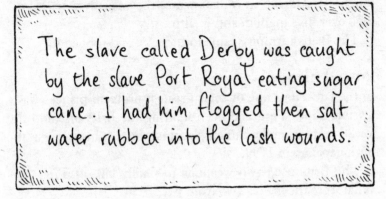

The slave called Derby was caught by the slave Port Royal eating sugar cane. I had him flogged then salt water rubbed into the lash wounds.

Incredible India

The Brits didn't have the empire idea all to themselves, of course. Spain, France and Holland wanted to grab some of this empire fortune. But the Brits found the secret of success ... a strong navy! That way they could defend all their colonies around the world – and attack the other countries!

Young Brits joined the army to see the world and fill their pockets with loot. At that time, India was made up of many small areas, each with its own wealthy ruler. They were often at war with each other, and when the Brits fought alongside an Indian prince he would reward them well. And when they fought AGAINST an Indian prince they usually won – and took over his kingdom and wealth.

The British Empire came to India ... and robbed it.

Potted prince

In the late 1700s one of their greatest problem princes was terrible Tipu. Tipu had been fighting the Brits on and off for 20 years when he came up against them at his fortress at Seringapatam in 1799.

The Brits used two weapons to finally kill off Tipu ... What were they? Pick two from five!

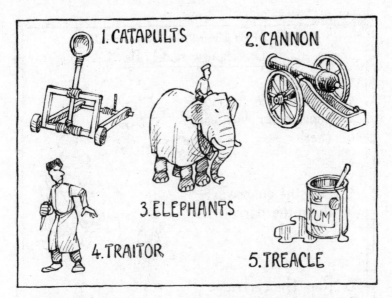

1. CATAPULTS
2. CANNON
3. ELEPHANTS
4. TRAITOR
5. TREACLE

Answer: **2** and **4**.

The cannon blasted a hole in the wall around Seringapatam while Tipu's traitor general let the Brits rush in.

Brave Tipu rushed to defend the hole in the wall. In spite of four deadly wounds he fought on till he was finally shot down. Tipu's body was found after the battle – under a pile of other bleeding corpses. Nasty!

Suffering sepoys

Indian soldiers (called 'sepoys') were brilliant fighters and the Brits used them all over the world. Yet the British managed to upset these super soldiers. In 1857 the sepoys mutinied against their Brit officers. Why?

Bullets. The Brits gave the sepoys new rifles with 'cartridges'. These cartridges had gunpowder under a paper cover. To load you had to…

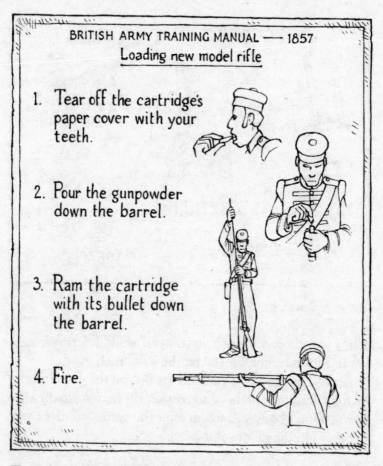

BRITISH ARMY TRAINING MANUAL — 1857

Loading new model rifle

1. Tear off the cartridge's paper cover with your teeth.

2. Pour the gunpowder down the barrel.

3. Ram the cartridge with its bullet down the barrel.

4. Fire.

To make the bullet slide down (3), the cartridge was covered with grease. Of course that meant that you'd get grease in your mouth when you bit off the paper cover (1).

The sepoys were not Christians like the Brit officers. They were mostly Hindu and Muslim. The Hindus were not allowed to touch cows (because they were sacred) and the Muslims were not allowed to touch pigs (because they were filthy).

So it should have been simple for the Brits. All they had to remember was: 'Do NOT use grease made from the fat of cows OR pigs.' Easy!

What did the Brits do? They used grease made from the fat of cows and pigs!*

The sepoys rebelled, of course. Brit women and children were massacred at Kanpur and the Brit revenge was brutal.

- Muslim mutineers were sewn into PIG skins before they were hanged – a horror worse than death.
- Mutineers were forced to clean up the blood from their massacre – and if they refused they were lashed and made to lick it up.

After the Kanpur massacre the nervous Brits punished anyone on the slightest excuse. One Brit soldier boasted …

I seed two Indians talking on a cart. Soon I hear one of them say 'Kanpur'. I knowed what that meant. So I fetched Tom Walker and he heard 'em say 'Kanpur', and we knowed what that meant. So we polished them both off.

* Actually some historians say the Brits did no such thing and that the pig-fat/cow-fat story was invented by trouble-makers.

Empress's quick eastern quiz

As well as being India's great white empress, Queen Victoria also ruled over a vast Eastern Empire. Here she is, with her deceased husband, to ask you some quick questions...

47

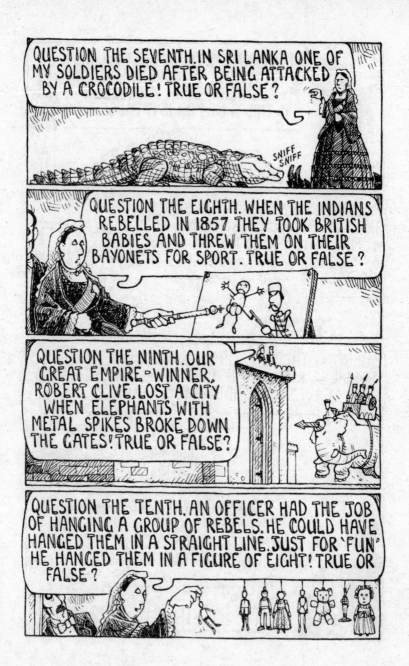

DO YOU HAVE THE ANSWERS, ALBERT?

Answers:

1 True. The Burmese had some customs that the British just didn't understand. An American visitor said in 1824 that:

The Burmese people are a simple-minded, lazy people. They are honest and polite, very generous to strangers. They like a quiet life, smoking and gossiping and sleeping through the day and listening to wild music and singing through half the night.

Does that remind you of anyone in your class at school?

2 False. The Thuggees had their own secret code and 'Pass the tobacco' actually meant 'Strangle him now!' The Thuggees got away with so many murders because they were ordinary villagers most days but ruthless killers when they joined a party of travelling strangers. Thuggees hardly ever killed British travellers though.

3 True. The Afghan Nikkuls thought John Nicholson was a god! He had great power – when an Afghan prince spat at Nicholson's feet, Nich made him lick it up! Britain never conquered the rest of the Afghans. The fierce tribesmen vanished into their mountain hide-outs. They attacked British supply columns, cut telegraph wires or picked off small patrols. They crept up to towns and attacked army families at night. As Colonel Hutchinson said calmly in the 1898 fighting:

It is extremely unpleasant, this whiz and spatter of bullets while you are at dinner or trying to enjoy a pipe round a camp fire before you go to bed!

4 False. It's what the Burmese *believed*, but in fact the holy woman was shot dead during the battle! Two British soldiers were kidnapped by the Burmese in 1824 and that gave the Brits the excuse to invade. 3,586 British troops captured Rangoon – but by 1826, the end of the war, 3,115 of those men had died in Burma. Only 150 of them died in battles – the rest died from diseases like cholera. The war cost Britain £13 million but the victory added another fat chunk to the Empire.

5 True. The Indian Mutiny broke out in 1857 when Indian soldiers in the British Army revolted. The British soldiers were trapped in the northern Indian city of Lucknow for several months (which is why they ran out of tobacco). Not a day went by without a death. The Indians dug mines under the city walls of Lucknow and blew them up – but the first one was too short and they just blew a hole in the ground outside the walls. Somebody couldn't measure! In the end more British soldiers came and rescued the trapped troops.

6 False. More died of disease than battle. But at one time the biggest killer of all was booze! The army boozer was open all day and the men could buy almost two litres of rum for 10p. An officer in India said…

There were men dying every day from drink which did more for death than fever!

HE'LL LIKE IT HERE

WHY?

HE'S AMONGST SPIRITS

Drunken soldiers were often arrested by Indian police using a neat weapon. The Indian police carried nets! They threw them over the drunk's head, knocked him off his feet and rolled him up! Then he was carted back to his army camp. Why don't teachers use that on school bullies?

7 True. A troop of British soldiers was marching by a river when a crocodile appeared and fancied a bit of Brit. The man died and his mates took their revenge by shooting any crocs they saw. (At least they weren't short of food.)

WAITER! BRING ME A CROCODILE SANDWICH – AND MAKE IT SNAPPY!

8 False … probably. When the Indian soldiers rebelled against their British rulers they massacred British women and children. British newspapers showed drawings of the Indians throwing babies on their bayonets, but these pictures were meant to stir up British horror and they aren't proof that it actually happened.

9 False. Robert Clive was a rogue who won lots of India for Britain – and made himself a fortune, of course. He captured the city of Arcot in 1751. Indian armies surrounded the city and they sent elephants with spikes on their heads to batter down the gates. Clive's defenders shot at the elephants with muskets. That didn't kill the poor jumbos – but it made them very angry! So the elephants charged *the other way* and trampled hundreds of Indians. Clive 'saved' Arcot.

(By the way, what is the difference between an African elephant and an Indian elephant? About 3,000 miles!)
10 True. The Brits who took revenge on Indian rebels were among the most blood-thirsty in the bloody history of Britain.

Dreadful down under

In 1788 six shiploads of convicts arrived at Port Jackson in Australia. 570 men and 160 women stepped ashore while the native Aborigine people shouted 'Warra! Warra!' at them.

Talk Aborigine

But what does 'Warra! Warra!' mean?
a) G'day! G'day!
b) Funny people! Funny people!
c) Go away! Go away!

Answer:
c) The Aborigines were not pleased to see the British convicts land. They thought they looked like bad news – and they were right!

Little terror

Of these first convicts the youngest was how old?
a) nineteen b) fifteen c) nine

Answer:

c) John Hudson was a nine-year-old chimney sweep. He must have felt a bit lost, poor kid! After all, there weren't a lot of chimneys in Australia in those days. He'd have to get a new job – kangaroo-pouch-sweep, maybe?

The oldest convict was Dorothy Handland and her job in England had been a rag dealer. Dorothy was 88 years old and it's amazing she survived that journey of 36 *weeks*! forty-eight of the other convicts had died on the journey.

Terrifying Tasmania

The Aborigines of Tasmania had lived on their island, cut off from Australia, for 12,000 years. They were Stone Age people, but they got along well enough, and up to 20,000 lived on the island when the Brits arrived in 1802. Eighty years later there were NONE.

Where did these simple (and fairly harmless) people go? They were wiped out by a Great British idea.

Of course there were convicts at Port Jackson in Australia. But how could you punish a really rotten convict who kept breaking the laws – a sort of 'super-convict'? Why not send him (or her) to Tasmania! No need to build a prison – just dump the convicts on the island and let them wander round to live or die...

...OR KILL

These wandering criminals were known as 'bushrangers' and they brought terror to the natives of Tasmania ... the Aborigines. The bushrangers killed the Aborigines as if it were a game. Aborigine men were tied to trees and used for target practice. As one brutal bushranger said...

I'd shoot an Aborigine as easily as I'd shoot a sparrow. And at the same time I get a lot of fun from this sort of sport!

But they didn't stop there. A witness reported...

One bushranger, known as Carrots, killed an Aborigine man. Then he seized the dead man's wife. He cut off the man's head and fastened it round the wife's neck. Then he drove the weeping woman off to his den to be his slave.

55

Many Aborigine women were kept as slaves and chained in the bushranger homes till they were needed for work. One bushranger claimed...

Whenever I want her for anything I take a burning stick from the fire and press it on her skin!

But there was one cruelty that shocked even the other bushrangers. A baby was snatched from its mother and buried alive in the ground up to its neck. Believe me, you would NOT want to know what was done to the baby's head...

The savage snobs

The convicts had a small excuse for their evil behaviour...

WE CONVICTS HAVE TRAVELLED HALFWAY ROUND THE WORLD WHILE OUR FRIENDS AND FAMILIES DIED ON THE SHIPS; WE ARE FLOGGED AND STARVED. WE HAVE TO BE HARD TO SURVIVE. BUT WHAT ABOUT THE POSH FOLK? EH? WHAT ABOUT THEM?

The convicts shared the island with the governors and their families who lived as grandly as they did back in Britain. In some posh areas of Tasmania the ladies and gentlemen hunted Aborigines for 'sport'. If one of these ladies had written a letter home it may have looked like this…

Risden
Tasmania
24 July 1821

Darling Mummy,
Here we are in this awful country. I am so bored most of the time. But yesterday we had some sport. I prepared a picnic for my dear Gerald and we set off with a bunch of friends into the bush to hunt the natives. We took the hunting dogs with us to sniff them out. Usually the dogs chase the natives out of the bush and the chaps shoot them down as they run.

Yesterday the sport wasn't so good. But clever Gerald had thought of that! He'd brought with us a native woman prisoner. He set her free to run home and she made a wonderful target for the bullets!

Did I tell you, Gerald has a barrel of vinegar? Every time he kills a native he cuts off the ears and pickles them in the barrel. Clever old Gerald has almost filled the barrel!

And my Gerald is so witty! Last week he took two pistols from the house – one was loaded and one was not. He found a friendly native and showed him the pistols. Then Gerald placed the empty pistol to his own head and pulled the trigger – of course it clicked, but nothing happened. Then he gave the loaded pistol to the native and told him to do the same. The simple chap blew his brains out against a tree trunk! Laugh? I nearly <u>wept</u> with laughter.

Of course the natives sometimes fight back and burn the settlers' houses. But then the army go after them and destroy them. The local newspaper said, 'For every British settler they

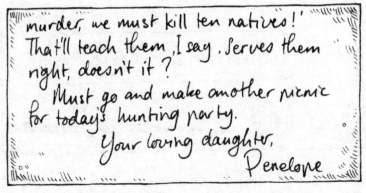

murder, we must kill ten natives!'
That'll teach them, I say. Serves them
right, doesn't it?
    Must go and make another picnic
for today's hunting party.
        Your loving daughter,
                Penelope

This letter is made-up but the stories in it are all terribly true.

The end
The Tasmanian Aborigines were vanishing.

- More Aborigines died of diseases the British brought and the tribes shrank.
- Settlers spread across the island and the British cattle replaced the Aborigines' kangaroos so the Aborigines starved. The tribes shrank again.
- The long-suffering natives finally stopped having children altogether and that eventually made the tribes die out entirely.
- Some Aborigines even began to slaughter their own children ... babies can get in the way when you are fighting to survive.

In 1832 a 'kind' British Christian had 220 Aborigines shipped off to Flinders Island where they could make themselves a nice new home – except the Island was a bleak, cold place. The Aborigines could see their old home, Tasmania, across the water but they could never return. It's said that many died of home-sickness.

In 1869 the last native Tasmanian man, King Billy, died of poisoning from drinking too much alcohol. But STILL the brutal Brits wouldn't let him rest. They wanted to study his body! So a surgeon...

- cut off his head.
- skinned the head and placed the skin on another skull.
- sent the head back to Britain.

Others cut off King Billy's hands and finally the whole body was stolen from the grave.

As you can imagine, the last woman, Truganini, was worried the same would happen to her corpse. She died in 1876, the last native Tasmanian. To save her being chopped and changed she was buried inside the walls of a prison. The plan didn't work though, and her bones ended up on display in Hobart Museum, Tasmania.

The Brutal Brits had wiped out an entire race in just 70 years. Here's how...

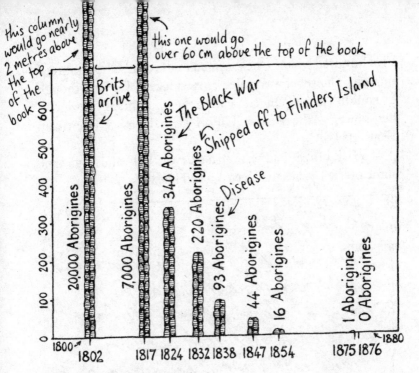

this column would go nearly 2 metres above the top of the book →

this one would go over 60 cm above the top of the book

Brits arrive

The Black War

Shipped off to Flinders Island

Disease

20000 Aborigines

7,000 Aborigines

340 Aborigines

220 Aborigines

93 Aborigines

44 Aborigines

16 Aborigines

1 Aborigine 0 Aborigines

1800 1802 1817 1824 1832 1838 1847 1854 1875 1876 1880

Nasty New Zealand

Meanwhile, across in New Zealand the Brits *failed* to wipe out the natives, the Maoris.

The Brit settlers used a common trick. They made peace with the natives then got the natives to sign over the land to Queen Victoria. The Brits gave the Maoris booze and guns – the Maoris gave the Brits New Zealand. In the words of the old British proverb…

FAIR EXCHANGE IS NO ROBBERY

Five hundred Maori chiefs agreed to the deal! One disagreed though. The rebel was called Hone Heke Pokai, and though he couldn't attack Queen Victoria, he *could* attack the sign of her power – the British Union Jack flag that flew from Flagstaff Hill.

If a Brit officer had written a diary of 1844 and 1845 then some of the entries may have looked like this...

20 July 1844

There was a Maori raid on Kororareka. Chief Heke attacked Kororareka to rescue a Maori girl who was living with the local British butcher. She didn't even want to be rescued, poor girl!! She used to be one of Heke's servants and she always called Heke 'Pig's head'. No one was hurt in the raid – but oddly one of Heke's friends chopped down our flag-pole!

17 August 1844

Our new flag-pole stood proudly on Flagstaff Hill – until this morning.

Some Maori's sneaked up and chopped it down – again! It's guarded by 170 soldiers sent from Australia. We can't let sneaky Heke get away with it! Victoria's flag shall fly!

9 September 1844

New flag-pole chopped down a third time. This is beyond a joke! Britannia rules the waves and Britons never, never, never shall have their flags flattened. Captain Fitzroy has a marvellous plan to nobble the natives He is taking a huge old ship's mast – thick as a tree trunk! The Maoris can attack it, but it will take them so long to chop down we'll have the army there to stop them. The post is defended by a small fort. That's the end of horrible Heke's game!

11 March 1845

Disaster! The flag-pole is down! The men at the fort were digging ditches when Heke's men leapt on them and massacred them with their knives and coral-studded clubs. Maoris also attacked the town and set it on fire. The biggest explosion was in the gunpowder dump – not caused by the Maoris, but by a British workman with a careless spark from his pipe! I always thought smoking was bad for your health. We British retreated to the safety of a warship – six men who returned were hacked down. Final score, 19 British settlers dead and 29 wounded.

Rotten revenge

Of course the Brits sent in the army to get revenge. The band played 'Rule Britannia' as they landed. The British soldiers had the help of the friendly Maoris plus some 'pakeha' Maoris – British men who had gone to live with the natives. Men like Jackey Marmon, an ex-convict, who said he had…

- Slaughtered rival Maoris in battle and
- Eaten them at cannibal feasts!

Jackey could have been lying about noshing on natives. But

it *was* true that a dead British soldier was found with neat pieces of meat sliced off his legs. Perhaps Jackey's Maori friends *did* eat people from time to time.

The Brits finally defeated Heke but only by treachery. The Maoris had become Christians and thought Sunday was a day of peace. The Brits (who were also supposed to be Christians) attacked on a Sunday when the Maoris were praying. (Which was a bit of a cheat! A bit like taking a football penalty kick while the goalkeeper is blowing his nose.)

And that flag-pole? Heke died of a disease in 1850, six years after he started flattening flag-poles – but while he lived that flag-pole was never raised again. So who won? No one. Who lost? As usual, everyone.

Awful for animals

As they explored the world the British found plenty of new and exciting animals to kill and even sometimes exterminate. The British Empire was certainly awful to animals.

> *HORRIBLE HISTORIES HEALTH WARNING:*
> Do not read this if you are an animal lover.

Evil for elephants

African elephants had a bad time once the Brits arrived. They were simply massacred for their tusks. Why did the people of Britain need so many tusks? For something important? Oh, yeah!

They were used for…

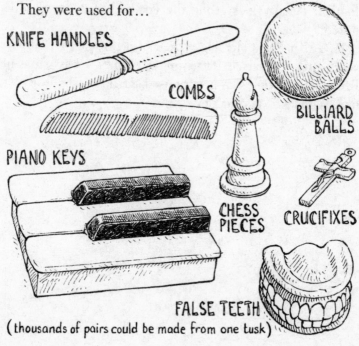

KNIFE HANDLES

COMBS

BILLIARD BALLS

PIANO KEYS

CHESS PIECES

CRUCIFIXES

FALSE TEETH
(thousands of pairs could be made from one tusk)

Some tusks were so large that they were used as door posts in houses.

Indian elephants – the ones with the smaller ears – were used by the Brits to move logs. They could be very clever, the Brits discovered. One elephant was said by an eye-witness to be especially clever…

As he passed a water pipe, feeling that he wanted a drink, he turned on the tap with the tip of his trunk and drank his fill and then went on, leaving the tap running. His owner said that it was his one bad habit. He always forgot to turn the tap off again!

Cute! But not as clever as this elephant…

A transport elephant was carrying a load of tents across a river when it got its feet into a quicksand. It immediately seized with its trunk, one after another, three natives who were walking alongside it and pushed them down under its feet to gain a foothold. This was

> intelligent of it but was a thing
> that wasn't done in the best
> elephantine circles and the poor
> thing was condemned to wear
> heavy chain bracelets round each
> foot for the rest of its life.

The punishment for another extraordinary elephant was even more cruel…

> Once when we had twenty elephants
> in camp one of these had a grudge
> against its driver and, seeing him
> asleep in the midday rest time,
> it put out its foot to stamp on
> him but made a bad shot and
> only crushed his thigh.
>
> There was an immense hullabaloo
> and the offending elephant was
> taken by the other drivers and
> tied to a tree. The remaining
> nineteen elephants were then
> formed up and told of the offence
> committed by number Twenty and
> were invited to give him a hiding.

> *This they did. Each elephant, taking a length of chain in its trunk, marched past in single file behind the culprit, and each, as he went by, slung the chain round with tremendous force on to his hind parts.*

Ouch!

Hideous for hippos

Life wasn't much fun for cute, cuddly hippos once the Brits arrived in Africa. The Brits liked to kill them (for fun, not because the Brits were hungry or in danger). Here's how...

- Lie by a watering-hole and watch where the hippo raises its eyes and nose.
- Aim your rifle at the spot.
- The hippo will always shove up his snout in the same spot.
- When he does it again, fire!

A hippo killed this way once made a great treat for Robert Baden-Powell's men. He described the feast they had.

You should have seen our natives and what they did with that hippo. As a first step they cut a square hole in his side, just big enough to admit a man's hand.

One man went in with a knife and fetched out all sorts of tit-bits in the way of chunks of liver, heart, etc, which he handed to his friends.

Of all the horrible sights you could imagine that grinning native, literally covered with blood from head to foot, was a complete picture.

By nightfall there were nearly a hundred natives collected on the carcass and to these people a lump of raw meat gives as much joy as a whole plum pudding would to a boy at Christmas.

Except you don't usually eat plum pudding raw ... with the blood running out as you munch it. And that's what that group did! Yeuch!

Deadly for dogs

Wherever the British army went, dogs went with them. Some of the mad mutts seemed to 'adopt' the soldiers. Sadly this was a mistake – if they picked the losing side! Look what happened in Maiwand, Afghanistan, in 1880…

The Brits were fighting the Afghans … and losing. There were just 11 Brits left in a ruined town. They were surrounded by Afghans and the Afghans were waving knives at them … the Brits would be cruelly chopped up if they were taken alive, so they fought on. An Afghan officer described their end…

These men charged from the shelter of a garden and died with their faces to the enemy, fighting to the death. So fierce was their charge, and so brave their actions, no Afghan dared to approach to cut them down. So, standing in the open, back to back, firing steadily, every shot counting, surrounded by thousands, these British soldiers died. It was not until the last man was shot down that the Afghans dared to advance on them. The behaviour of those last eleven was the wonder of all who saw it.

71

Stirring stuff. But it wasn't just the soldiers who died at Maiwand. The army was a 'family' and, like most families, it had its pets – dogs. And the dogs fought and wounded any Afghans daft enough to get too close! So the dogs had to die too.

One British captain and his dog died together. The Afghans buried the man and then, as an insult, threw his dog into his grave too. But the Victorian Brits didn't see it as an insult! They saw it as two brave fighters resting in peace, side by side.

The good news is that a dog called Bobbie survived the same battle. Bobbie was a small, woolly, white dog with a brown face and brown ears on top of his flat head. His master, Sergeant Kelly, fought and fell with the Last Eleven. Bobbie fought on and was chopped with a sword.

Brave Bobbie got up and limped off to return to his home fort – 50 miles away! He survived and returned to Britain and fame.

Bobbie was dressed in a red jacket and presented to the queen. Dog-loving Vic examined his wounds and pinned the Afghan War medal on his jacket.

Happy ending? Not really. Bored Bobbie strayed from the army camp in Gosport and got run over by a cab. You can still see his stuffed body in his Royal Berkshire regiment's museum in Salisbury … if looking at dead dogs is a hobby of yours!

Did you know…?
Brit army officers in India took a pack of fox-hounds over to steaming-hot India … to hunt jackals. But India was so hot the fox-hounds all died. (The jackals probably had a bit of a party!)

Gruesome games and sick sports

The Empire let Brits try new games they hadn't imagined before. Games like hog-hunting (aka 'pig-sticking'), which is great fun ... unless you happen to be a pig.

Brutal for boars

The pigs were 'wild boars' and they were hunted by wildly boring men like Robert Baden-Powell (the chap who is remembered today because he invented the Boy Scouts). This is how Lord Robert Baden-Powell described hog-hunting ...

The Boar

The boar is brave and tough, as fast as a horse, and can jump where a horse cannot. He stands as high as a table, is long in the leg, and very muscular. He doesn't hesitate to swim a river, even when it is inhabited by crocodiles.

Well, that is the fellow we hunt in India on horseback with spears, and there is no sport can touch hog-hunting for excitement or valuable training.

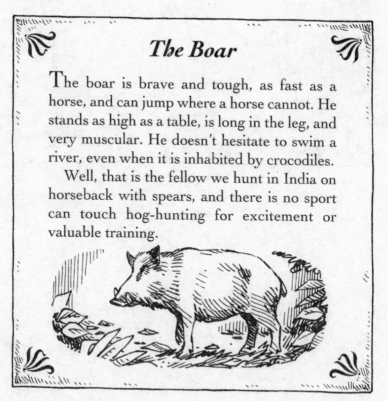

The Hunt

Three or four riders form a 'party'. Beaters drive the pig out of his lair in the jungle, and the party then race after him, but for the first three-quarters of a mile he can generally outrun them. The honours then go to the man who can first catch and spear him. But as soon as the boar finds himself in danger of being overtaken he either 'jinks', that is, darts off sideways, or else turns round and charges his pursuer.

A spear-thrust, unless delivered in a vital spot, has little effect beyond making him more angry, and then follows a good deal of charging on both sides, and it is not always the boar that comes off second best. He has a wonderful power of quick and effective use of his tusks and many a good horse has been fatally gashed by the animal he was hunting.

Hang on, Lord Bleedin-Trowell!. The poor *horse* wasn't hunting the boar! *You* were!

Chief Scout Robert obviously had some funny ideas about 'sport' – look at his idea of killing a hyena…

Big Game

I also had a ride after a hyena with a number of Arabs, one of the most alarming games I ever took part in, for the plan was to gallop him down and surround him and for every man then to loose off his rifle at him.

As we were in a circle we were firing inwards and towards each other, but fortunately, being mounted, the guns were pointed downwards and the many bullets which missed the hyena went into the sand.

A gang of men shooting at an exhausted hyena? Call that sport? Why not just go to the fairground and shoot at ducks?

Still, it was boars that Robert was mostly interested in. And when he wasn't murdering them he was adopting them! But even his pet baby-boar ended up pretty dead.

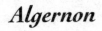

I was lucky enough to capture in the jungle a very young "squeaker," as young boars are called.

I took him home and kept him for a long time, and found him a delightful and interesting young friend. I got him to come to me when I called him for food.

There was an old stump of a tree in the garden around which Algernon (for that was his name) was never tired of galloping. He used to practise running a figure of eight round the stump, cutting at it with his baby tusks every time he passed, right and left alternately, thus practising for battles that were to come.

I had an old English horse loose in the field who, being a staunch pig-sticker, used to go for Algernon whenever she saw him. The little beggar loved leading her on till she tore after him, with ears back, eager to trample on him or to kick him if she could only get him.

Unfortunately one day some dogs about the place saw this chase going on and joined in and soon ran down poor little Algernon and bit and tore him so badly that he had to be killed. The killing was done with the spear as was right for his being a boar.

Never mind, Algernon would have made a good pork sausage. Why not try this recipe if your pet pig is ever attacked by dogs? It's for the Empire dish called 'Boudin'.

Recipe for Boudin

You need:
4 cups of pig blood
1 pound of pig fat
Some pig's intestines
1 cup of milk
4 onions
Mixed spices to taste
Salt and pepper

To make:
Mix the blood and milk.
Stir in the chopped pig fat, onions, spices, salt and pepper.

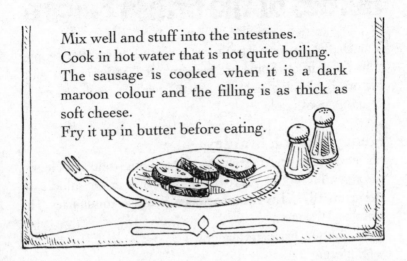

Mix well and stuff into the intestines.
Cook in hot water that is not quite boiling.
The sausage is cooked when it is a dark maroon colour and the filling is as thick as soft cheese.
Fry it up in butter before eating.

So, go on ... make a pig of yourself!

Did you know...?
In South Africa in 1879 the Brit soldiers found something they said was better than pig-sticking. A soldier described an attack by the Brits (on horses) on Zulu warriors (on foot)...

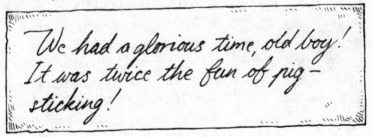

We had a glorious time, old boy! It was twice the fun of pig-sticking!

Heroes of the British Empire

The British Empire wasn't just a place – it was the people who lived in it. Some are remembered as heroes ... but history books don't always tell the terrible truth. *Horrible Histories* books do!

Henry Morton Stanley

Have you ever heard the story of Dr Livingstone and Henry Stanley? Those two great Brit heroes met in the middle of Africa in 1871. Livingstone was a Scottish missionary. He went to Africa to...

- teach the Christian religion.
- explore.
- stop African slavery.

Livingstone was the good guy. A true Brit hero. But there were no phones or faxes or e-mails in those days – just bicycle tyres and billiard balls* – so the Brit people didn't hear from Livingstone for a year or so.

That's when Henry Stanley set off to find dear David. Henry was a Welsh orphan who was adopted by a rich American, and who fought in the American Civil War – on both sides! In 1871 the American *New York Herald* newspaper paid Henry Stanley to get a great story – find Livingstone! Poor old Doctor Livingstone – he didn't even know he was lost!

* Hang on and you'll see why they became horribly historically important!

After walking hundreds of miles, through dozens of dangers, Stanley finally came across Livingstone and said those mega-cool words ... four of the most famous words in Brit Empire history...

DOCTOR LIVINGSTONE, I PRESUME

Of course Doc Dave SHOULD have said...

NO! I'M A MONKEY'S UNCLE YOU BRAIN-DEAD DINGBAT!

Instead, he said that other famous word in Brit Empire history ... 'Yes.'

Poor old Dave died a couple of years later. He was kneeling at his bed, as though he'd just been praying, when they found him. (But we don't know what his last prayer was. Probably, 'Please don't let me die!' or something.)

BUT ... Brit history books never go on to tell you what Henry Stanley did for the rest of his life. It was so horrible, teachers wouldn't dare tell you in case you throw up over your desk and they have to mop it up! So here goes – have the sick bucket handy...

Horrible Henry

Henry Stanley was hired by King Leopold of Belgium to help Belgium conquer the Congo area of Africa (the bit in the middle).

Bicycle tyres had been invented and the world would pay a fortune for the rubber that came from trees in the Congo. The world was also keen on ivory for billiard balls that grew on elephants in the Congo . . I mean the *ivory* grew on the elephants, not the billiard balls.

Horrible Henry set about his job with true Empire spirit – and a real talent for cruelty and greed. He was also a rotten racist. Here are the top ten terrors of his visit...

1 Secret slaves. King Leopold and HH told the world they were freeing the Africans from Arab slavers. In fact, working for HH and his Belgian bosses was worse than slavery. Men, women and children had to carry huge loads for their white masters – a seven-year-old child would have to carry 10-kilo loads all day through the steaming jungles. One visitor reported...

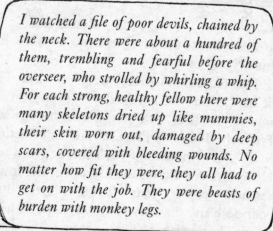

I watched a file of poor devils, chained by the neck. There were about a hundred of them, trembling and fearful before the overseer, who strolled by whirling a whip. For each strong, healthy fellow there were many skeletons dried up like mummies, their skin worn out, damaged by deep scars, covered with bleeding wounds. No matter how fit they were, they all had to get on with the job. They were beasts of burden with monkey legs.

They were fed on a handful of rice and stinking dried fish.

2 Cheerful chiquotte. The Africans of the Congo weren't slaves – they had a choice! They could produce enough rubber for Stanley's rubber farms – or face the chiquotte.

What's that? It's a specially cruel whip. If you fancy making one to try a 'Living History' lesson, with your teacher as the rubber collector, here's how…

The sharp edges meant the whip cut into the victim's skin.
- A few blows would leave you scarred for life.
- 25 lashes could knock you out.
- One hundred or more (quite common) would often kill you.

Finally the sufferer was expected to pick himself (or herself) up and give a military salute!

3 Fastened families. You don't want to work on the rubber farm? Fine … Stanley's men would hold your wife and children prisoner until you do. Or, even nastier, those children could be thrown into the jungle and left to be eaten by the animals. Or thrown on the plains to be baked to death by the scorching sun. No food for those poor kids…

NOT EVEN A BAKED BEAN FOR THE BAKED BEING

You'll be pleased to know HH himself went hungry from time to time. On a journey through the Ituri rainforest he and his 389 men ran out of food. They survived by eating roasted ants.

4 Grim guns. Stanley's men had guns, the Africans didn't. This made fighting a bit one-sided, especially as their favourite weapon was the machine-gun. But even the ordinary rifle could be used against troublemakers in a cruel way. One of Stanley's pitiless policemen boasted…

We surrounded the rebel camp and hid in the long grass. We watched the women as they crushed dried bananas to make flour. When we were ready I raised my rifle and shot one of the Africans clean through the chest. The game had started!

84

5 Handless horrors. Rebels had ears or noses sliced off. But worse was the way the police claimed their reward for capturing rebels – they chopped off an African's hand and were paid for every hand they collected. But there wasn't just an odd hand here and there – there were hundreds of hands and hundreds of bodies left to rot. At Lake Tumba, a Swedish missionary, E V Sjoblom wrote:

> I saw ... dead bodies floating on the lake with the right hands cut off, and the officer told me when I came back why they had been killed. It was all part of the war for rubber. When I crossed the stream I saw some dead bodies hanging down from the branches in the water. As I turned away my face at the horrible sight one of the native policemen said, 'Oh, that is nothing. A few days ago I returned from a fight, and I brought the white man 160 hands and they were thrown in the river.'

6 Terrible tricks. Stanley and his men used tricks to fool the Africans into signing over land to them.

- To make the Africans think they had magical powers, they attached batteries to their arms under their coats. When the white man grasped the black man's hand, the black man got an electric shock that nearly knocked him off his feet. (Don't try this on your grotty little brother at home!)
- Magnifying glasses were used to light cigars. The white man lied that he was a special friend of the sun, which lit his cigar. Then he threatened...

7 Pitiful prisoners. One village was captured, the people tied up and herded out. They were expected to carry heavy baskets that the soldiers gave them. The baskets contained food supplies ... and some contained smoked human flesh! Prisoners had to march very quickly. One woman was dragged out with a baby in her arms; the soldiers took her baby and threw it into the grass to die. A lot of men were killed on the way and just left where they dropped.

8 Horrible heads. A British explorer who passed through Stanley Falls in 1895 reported that many African men, women and children had been brought to the Falls and their heads had been used by Captain Rom (of the Police Force) as a decoration around the flower beds in front of his house.

One of HH's men shot a native for fun and had the dead African's head packed in a box of salt and returned to London to be stuffed and mounted in a glass case.

9 Painful for pygmies. The Congo pygmies were usually a peaceful tribe, but they could be wicked. Many practised slavery and cannibalism. They went to war with anyone – even other pygmy clans – and their favourite trophy of a battle was a severed head or hand. In 1906, a pygmy from the Congo named Ota Benga was delivered to the Bronx zoo in the USA where he was actually put on display in a cage with

an orang-utan. A group of African-American priests managed to get Benga released, and he stayed in the US until he killed himself ten years later.

10 Rich rewards. While Horrible Henry Stanley and King Leopold ruled the Congo half of the native people there died.

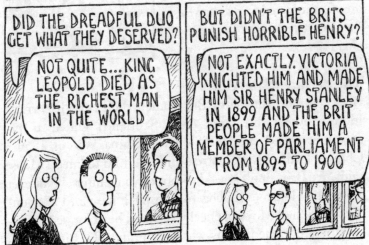

DID THE DREADFUL DUO GET WHAT THEY DESERVED?

NOT QUITE... KING LEOPOLD DIED AS THE RICHEST MAN IN THE WORLD

BUT DIDN'T THE BRITS PUNISH HORRIBLE HENRY?

NOT EXACTLY. VICTORIA KNIGHTED HIM AND MADE HIM SIR HENRY STANLEY IN 1899 AND THE BRIT PEOPLE MADE HIM A MEMBER OF PARLIAMENT FROM 1895 TO 1900

The only good news is he didn't get his dying wish – he wanted to be buried in Westminster Abbey next to the good Doctor Livingstone! In fact he was buried in Furze Hill in Surrey … and he still is.

Cool courage…

People in Britain believed their soldiers were better and braver than any other soldiers in the world – even when they got stuffed by the enemy! The British public loved tales of terrific courage. Some famously Cool Britannia heroes included…

The Light Brigade

At the battle of Balaclava (in the Ukraine) in 1856 the Light Brigade were ordered to charge at the Russian cannons. It was suicide. They did it and they died – and the horses became a bit of a mess too! Did anyone ask the horses if they wanted to charge?

The Private of the Buffs

Even common, dirty little Brit soldiers didn't give in. Private John Moyse (who came from Scotland) joined a Brit regiment called the Buffs. In the China War of 1860 a Chinese lord captured Moyse and told him to kneel. Moyse said, 'We Brits don't kneel in front of you Chinese! Not even a poor Brit like me will bow to a posh Chinese lord like you!' The Lord had Moyse's cheeky Scottish head lopped off.

Moyse became famous when Sir Francis Hastings Doyle

wrote a poem about him – 'The Private of the Buffs'. It said he was a true Brit – standing up to bullies even though it cost him his life! You wouldn't want to read the whole thing nowadays but a sharp sample goes…

The Private of the Buffs

And thus with eyes that would not shrink,
With knee to man un-bent,
Un-faltering on its dreadful brink,
To his red grave he went.

The poem should have been about using your head not losing your head! Something like this…

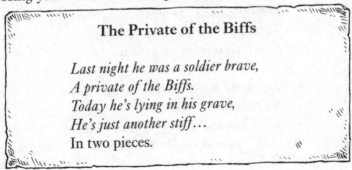

The Private of the Biffs

Last night he was a soldier brave,
A private of the Biffs.
Today he's lying in his grave,
He's just another stiff…
In two pieces.

He stood before the Chinese lord
And showed no drop of fear.
A British heart beat in his chest,
But no brain between his ears...
Or anywhere else for that matter.

'Just kneel down there!' the Chinese said
'Kneel down, I'll spare your neck!'
'I won't! Cos I'm a battling Brit!
I won't, I say, by heck!'
Oooops!

The Chinese lord he shrugged and sighed,
'You are a brain-dead Biff
To make me lop your silly head!'
The lord, you know, was miffed...
A bit put out.

So Private Moyse they took him out,
And made him dig a pit.
They knelt him down and chopped his head
The head fell straight in it...
And the body followed. Thump!

The sword was quick, so Private Moyse
No pain in his neck felt.
The Chinese lord he laughed and said,
'To get the chop ... he KNELT...
So I won!'

Moyse lost his head, his grave was red,
And don't you feel like blubbin'?
He didn't die for Britain's queen!
He died cos he was stubborn...
As a mule.

STIFF
BIFF

Did you know...?
The Chinese later said Private Moyse had died of drink! Perhaps mad Moyse's messy end was just a story? Private Moyse's boss, Captain Brabazon, *was* beheaded by the Chinese.

Dead brave

Dying bravely was seen as a 'British' thing to do. Yet the Brits admired their enemies who died bravely too ... so maybe it wasn't so 'British' after all! Brave enemies included...

- Tartar warriors in China who killed themselves in a Chinese temple rather than be captured alive.
- South African Zulus who fell in heaps as they ran at the Brit guns ... then stopped to pick up their dead friends and used them as shields! Would you do that to your friend? (Better not answer that!)

- Sind troops in India who attacked Brit guns with swords and were massacred, of course.

And talking of Sind, you need to know about the only Brit Empire joke ever invented! Brit General Sir Charles Napier captured Sind in February 1843. He sent a message back to Britain. It was the Latin word...

It means, 'I have sinned'. Get it? 'I have Sind!' Oh, never mind.

There are hundreds of examples of Brits mowing down native peoples – guns against spears. The Brits SAID they admired the courage of the enemy – but that didn't stop the massacres!

Popham's people

A Brit force attacked Buenos Aires in 1806 to 'free' the South American people from their rotten Spanish rulers. The Brit leader, Admiral Hope Popham, hoped to pop 'em off quickly. When the Brit soldiers attacked, Admiral Pop said...

They marched forward with all the cool courage that is the sign of the British soldier.

That was what the British soldier was supposed to be like. Cool and courageous – Old Pop should have added ... and 'cruel'. Here's why...

Admiral Popham had a problem with his Spanish prisoners of war. If he kept them they'd eat the food his men needed. If he set them free they'd join the Spanish friends and fight against him. So Popham abandoned the Spanish prisoners on a rock in the middle of the Rio Plate river.

JUST POPHAM ON THAT ISLAND

The Spanish prisoners had…
- no food.
- no fresh water.
- no shelter.

It would have been a slow death for the Spanish but for one thing … seals. Yes! Those cute, fluffy, furry, flabby, lovable little creatures! The Spanish were so pleased to see them! They smashed the seals to death, skinned them and made water-wings from the seal skins! Forty trapped prisoners used them to swim to safety!

YOUR FATE IS SEALED!

THAT PUN WOULDN'T WORK IN SPANISH!

NOPE

Did you know…?

The Brits could be pretty mean to their own soldiers. Men who stole or refused to obey an order could be whipped on

93

their bare back with a whip called a cat-o'-nine-tails. (It was called that because there were nine strings to the lash, not because it was made of dead cat.) The flogging could go on till the man was dead. Then, in 1829, the number of lashes was cut to just 500!

Food was usually dreadful. A soldier was paid 12 pence a day – then charged 6 pence for his food! But the most cruel charge of all was for the soldier who had to pay for his own coffin! The man fell sick when he was on duty in Australia and the doctor said he would die. The army carpenter made his coffin but then the man got better! The army still sent the soldier the bill, though! He paid it, but insisted that he keep the coffin in his room. It was fitted with shelves and held all his clothes neatly.

Nasty natives

The Brits battered people all around the world. But the natives could be pretty nasty too. They often had horrible habits that disgusted the Brits and may even disgust you! Here are a top evil eight with a disgustometer alongside...

Thuggees (India 1200-ish to 1840-ish)

96

Nasty note:

How is it religious to go around strangling people? Well…

- It's all because of this Kool Kali that the Thuggees worshipped. Modern pictures of her show her standing on a dead body.

- She has four arms, a necklace of 50 human skulls and a belt of human arms while she is holding an axe, a severed human head, a trident and a bowl of blood! (It's handy having four arms!) Her long tongue drips with the fresh blood of her enemies.

- The Thugs believed the old story that good Kali strangled evil Rukt Bij-dana at the dawn of time.

- Kali then created two humans from the sweat of her brow.

- Kali ordered the humans to worship her … but to strangle anyone who didn't worship her!

How did they manage to strangle travellers when the travellers MUST have known the dangers and been prepared? Well…

- The Thugs pretended to be travellers and mixed with them on the journey. These journeys were usually between November and May, the 'travelling season'.

- They were quick killers, using their silk scarves as a noose and attacking from behind – noose over the head, knee in the back and … Cccct! When they had time the Thuggees ate and slept among their victims' corpses.

- The Thugs cut the victims' bodies with holy gashes and then buried them – or threw them down wells, which made the water taste awful. They burned the things they didn't take with them so they left no traces: they were 'thuggee' … hidden.

How did the Brits get rid of these Kali killing, noose-knotting, goat-goring, scarf-stranglers? Well…

- In the 1830s Brits (led by a ruthless soldier, Colonel William Sleeman) managed to snatch some stranglers and offered a deal: 'Tell us who the other Thugs are and we'll spare your life.' One of Sleeman's jobs was to dig up the victims!

- Even the Thugs who told the truth were never set free! They were put in prison and had a tattoo on their bottom eyelid with the word 'Thug'.

- Thugs who didn't give up their wicked ways were hanged – but not with a nice silk scarf! By the 1840s most of the thuggery had ended. Not before time – a Thug named Buhram said he had strangled 931 people! (That must have stretched his silk scarf a bit!)

The Thugs are now gone from India but blood-dripping Kali is still one of India's most popular goddesses.

(Strange that the men we call 'thugs' today are usually football supporters … from Britain, waving scarves!)

DISGUSTOMETER RATING:

THE BUMPER BOOK OF SPORTS

No. 173: Lacrosse

You need:
A pitch about 100 metres by 60 metres.

A goal in a circle ten metres from each end of the pitch.

Two teams of ten. (Each player has a stick with a net on the end. If you haven't got lacrosse sticks then use a tadpole net.)

A ball. (Some people like to play lacrosse with a hard rubber ball about the size of a tennis ball. BUT it was said that some Canadian Indians used a human head instead of a ball. *The Bumper Book of Sports* does not advise this. A freshly chopped head will splatter blood and brains all over your strip, your face and the playing field – very slippery and dangerous. Of course you could use the head of a traffic warden – then you won't have a problem with splattered brains.)

RUBBER BALL   TENNIS BALL   DENNIS SMALL

To play:
Each team has a goalkeeper, three defenders, three midfielders and three attackers. There must always be four players in your own half and three in the enemy half.

99

Players can use their sticks to carry, catch or pass the ball and can kick it but not handle it.

Play four 15-minute quarters.

To score:
Pass the ball and shoot it into your opponents' net.
No tripping or hitting your opponents with your stick, but shoulder charges are allowed.

Nasty note:
The tale of the head for a ball may not be true – the Canadian Indians may have invented it to scare their enemies. But the following terrible tale *is* true. In 1763 the Brits had conquered Canada and a force of soldiers settled in Fort Michilimackinac. The Indians couldn't defeat the Brits while they sat in their fort, so they came up with a neat plan. They

said to the Brits, 'Say, you guys, would you like to come and watch us play lacrosse on the field outside the fort?' The Barmy Brits agreed. When the Indian players came close to the soldiers they threw away their lacrosse sticks and took out their tomahawks. Chop! Chop!

DISCUSTOMETER RATING:

Zulu Dingaan

From 1828 to 1838 a man called Dingaan was leader of the South African Zulu tribe – and Dingaan was not a nice man, as you'll discover in...

The *Horrible History* Zulu Quiz

Are you tough enough to be a Zulu chief like Dingaan? Just answer these simple questions and check your score. . .

1 How would you get to be Zulu chief in the first place?

a) Go down to the local job centre and fill in a form.

b) Be born a prince and wait patiently for your older brother, the king, to die.

c) Be born a prince and murder your brother, the king.

2 For most rulers, it's important to show off. How would you show the world you are a great Zulu chief?

a) Have jesters and dwarfs to entertain your guests.

b) Have lots of fat women for wives.

c) Have jesters, dwarfs AND loads of fat wives.

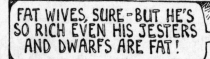

FAT WIVES, SURE – BUT HE'S SO RICH EVEN HIS JESTERS AND DWARFS ARE FAT!

3 Being top dog isn't all work and no play. How would you like to entertain yourself as Zulu chief?

a) Play football with your mates.

b) Hunt lions and other dangerous animals.

c) Have a palace glutton eat a whole goat for you.

BRAVO!

I HOPE HE DOESN'T WANT AN ENCORE

4 A friendly white Boer settler has returned 700 lost cattle to you – and cattle are a sign of wealth. How do you reward him?

a) Give him 70 cattle and two of your fat wives.

b) Spit on him and send him away with nothing.

c) Get him and his followers drunk, and kill them.

5 If you decide the man and his followers must die, how would you kill them?

a) Quickly and cleanly with a sharp chop of the axe while they are drunk and asleep.

b) Wait till they are awake and hang them.

c) Tie them up, take them to the Hill of Execution, bash their heads with clubs, then stick sharp wooden poles through their bodies from underneath. Let the man who helped you watch his followers die, then kill him last. Cut out his heart and liver.

6 You have 10,000 warriors. You come across a band of 460 white settlers at Blood River. What do you do to this pathetic mob of white men?

a) Spare their miserable lives.

b) Capture them and make them your slaves.

c) Attack and try to kill them all.

Answers:

Count the numbers of a), b) and c) answers. See which you have the most of.

Mostly a) – Sorry. You are a wimp. You will never be a tough cookie like Dingaan. You're more of a Dingbat. Get a soft job. Infant school teacher may suit you.

Mostly b) – You are not a very nice person. People who steal dummies from babies are nicer than you! But you still aren't tough as old Dingaan.

Mostly c) – Each c) answer is what Dingaan actually did. If you'd do the same you'd make a great Zulu leader ... just don't come near me, you nasty pastie!

But Dingaan's cruelty didn't do him any good. When his 10,000 Zulus attacked the 460 white settlers, the Zulus lost! There were 3,000 dead Zulus on the battlefield at Blood River – and just *two* dead settlers! Dingaan fled for his life and found safety in Swaziland. That's where he was murdered – by his own people. It's hard to feel sorry for him, isn't it?

DISGUSTOMETER RATING:

Zulu Shaka

If you think Dingaan was bad you would NOT like to meet the brother he killed – Shaka, who ruled from 1816 till 1828! Here are some foul facts about Shaka's life. But, *beware* – one of these facts is not true. Which one?

a) Before Shaka was born his mother said, 'The swelling in my stomach is just ishaki!' And 'ishaki' means 'a bad gut'. When the baby was born he was named ishaki (or Shaka) – so his name meant 'bad gut'.

b) Shaka and his mother were sent away from the Zulu nation. Life was hard, and they spent some time living in a cave, so Shaka grew up tough. Other boys picked on him, poor lad, because his naughty bits weren't very large. He grew up to be a big youth (though his naughty bits stayed a bit on the small side) and returned to the Zulu to lead them – so the first thing he had to do was kill the chief ... his own father. Would *you* kill your dad? (Better not answer that!)

c) Shaka was a great warrior chief – but a bit odd. For a start he was afraid of growing old and he was afraid a son would grow up to kill him. We can guess why he was worried about that! He had 1,200 wives but didn't want to be a father – so, if one of his wives got pregnant he murdered her! His 1,200 mothers-in-law must have been annoyed!

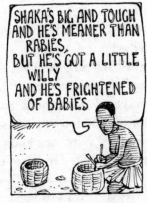

SHAKA'S BIG AND TOUGH AND HE'S MEANER THAN RABIES, BUT HE'S GOT A LITTLE WILLY AND HE'S FRIGHTENED OF BABIES

d) Shaka's mum died and he was really upset. Really REALLY upset. So he had 7,000 antelopes slaughtered for her funeral.

e) Shaka invented new weapons – a short stabbing-spear and a tough cow-skin shield. He also invented a new way of fighting. His army split into three and attacked the enemy from left, right and centre. Before Shaka invented this way of fighting, the Zulu warriors would just throw their long spears and run. Shaka made them sprint up to the enemy and stab – and it worked well in Shaka's day. Sadly it didn't seem to work so well when the Zulu came up against machine-guns 50 years later.

f) Shaka banned soldiers from wearing shoes. (Try saying 'Shaka scraps soldiers' shoes!' with a mouthful of mushrooms.) He made his army give up their sandals and toughen their feet so they could run faster – up to 50 miles a day!

g) Shaka punished any cowardly soldier with death. He also had them executed if they forgot to bring their spear to practice! (Imagine if there was death every time someone forgot their towel for school swimming lessons!) Shaka's soldiers were not allowed to have girlfriends either. The punishment? Death, of course.

h) Between 1815 and 1828, Shaka destroyed all the tribes in southern Africa that were opposed to him. This jolly time became known as Mfecane … or 'The Terror'. He probably caused the deaths of a MILLION people – that, readers, is totally terrible terror.

i) Shaka seemed to enjoy being cruel. After he killed someone he had a little catch-phrase you may like to copy. He shouted…

NGADLA!

You don't need me to tell you what that means! You do? Oh, all right then. It means, 'I have eaten!'

j) Shaka punished the Zulus after his mother died – he said they weren't sorry enough! His people had almost starved to death and he wasn't a popular lad any longer. Plots were plotted. But Shaka trusted his half-brothers, Dingaan and Mhlangane, and met them for a chat. They turned on him and hacked him to death. As he fell he said some great last words...

BROTHERS! WHAT HAVE I DONE?

That's what you call a really good question. Sadly, he didn't live long enough to hear the answer. Mighty Shaka's body was thrown in an empty grain pot (corny, but true). It was then filled with stones.

Answer:
d) is not true. When Shaka's mother died he didn't slaughter thousands of antelopes – he slaughtered thousands of PEOPLE. Shaka said...

I am upset. I want every family to know how upset I am so I am going to kill someone from every family! Doesn't that sound fair?

107

It's reckoned 7,000 people died because Shaka's mother died!

DISGUSTOMETER RATING:

Smoking, choking Chinese

Through the early 1800s the Brits in India were making a fortune selling drugs to the Chinese. The drug was a pain-killer called opium, and the Chinese smoked the stuff till they became addicts. Many smoked far too much and killed themselves.

The Chinese emperor tried to ban the Brit dope dealers so the British government went to war with him. They wanted their drug dealers to carry on making money from the opium misery.

Of course the Brits had better weapons than the Chinese and were happy to massacre them! On 10 March 1842 the Chinese even accidentally helped the Brits to massacre them at Ningpo town! There were two reasons: **1)** The Chinese were superstitious about tigers and **2)** the Chinese leaders spoke Mandarin Chinese while the Army leaders didn't. This is what happened...

The order went out from the Mandarin leaders…

It was not really a good idea to attack Ningpo because the Chinese knew the Brits were ready for them. But the Chinese believed all the tigers would help them!

Unfortunately, they didn't translate the rest of the Mandarin order properly. What it really said was…

What they thought it said was…

They left their guns behind and tried to attack Brit muskets and cannon using knives. No contest. The second wave of attackers had to climb over the corpses of the first wave. A British reporter said...

> There were so many corpses piled outside Ningpo's west gate that blood ran down the gutters.

The Chinese had no more luck at Chen-hai later that year. The problem was, the Chinese commander was drugged out of his mind with smoking opium – the stuff he was fighting to stop!

So what tricks did the nasty natives get up to when they fought the Brits? The usual fairly average cruelty...

- A British opium dealer was captured and executed by being strangled.

- British sailors were thrilled to see red boxes floating in the river. These were the boxes that posh Chinese ladies used to keep their rich fur and silk clothes in! A great present for the girlfriends back home, the sailors must have thought. They flung open the lids ... and the bombs inside went off.

- British troops who strayed outside their camp were executed ruthlessly. Captain Stead let his ship land at the wrong harbour. He was taken ashore, tied to a post and skinned alive.
- Chinese defenders fought ferociously but if they looked like losing they would often slit the throats of their own wives and children to stop then becoming Brit prisoners. Then they would hang themselves from the rafters. This even sickened a tough Brit soldier who wrote…

When the Chinese could no longer stand against us they drove their wives and children into wells or ponds, then destroyed themselves. In many houses there were eight to twelve dead bodies and I myself saw a dozen women and children drowning themselves in a small pond the day after the fight.

- A Chinese soldier cut his wife's throat with a rusty sword and threw his children down the garden well. But then he changed his mind and bandaged her up again and pulled the kids out – alive! She was not a happy woman!
- One Chinese soldier had his life spared by an Irish soldier who took him prisoner instead. The Chinese soldier was not pleased. He drew his knife and started to cut his own throat before the Irishman stopped him!

One Brit commander, Sir Hugh Gough, wrote…

I am sick at heart of war.

In 1842 the Chinese made peace, gave the British $21 million and they also gave them Hong Kong. But the Brits went on selling opium, and the Chinese went on smoking it … and dying.

DISGUSTOMETER RATING:

Bad in Benin

The American invention, the Maxim gun, fired ten bullets every second and helped Britain rule over the Empire. Troublemakers were attacked and had no chance. As the witty wallies said at the time…

Whatever happens,
We have got
The Maxim gun …
And they have not!

The Brits used the Maxim gun like a teacher used to use the cane – to teach someone a lesson! That's what happened in Benin, West Africa, in 1897.

The Brits had been worried about Benin ever since they came across it in the early 1800s. They didn't like the way the Benin people behaved. According to the Brits, the Ju-ju religion was cruel and humans were sacrificed. One Brit witness said…

The truth is probably that the executed men were criminals and the beheading wasn't as cruel as the public hangings that were happening back in Britain at that time! The Brits also said …

- the Benin Oba (king) was a slave trader and he had to be stopped.
- in 1886 Benin natives attacked British servants, took them to Sacrifice Island, executed them … and then ate them.
- in 1896 Oba Overami chained criminals to a building where their ears were sliced off with a razor.
- Oba Overami also had the path to his palace littered with 40 rotting corpses, skulls and human bones to show his power.

But Oba Overami was guilty of the greatest crime of all … he didn't want to be ruled by the Brits or be part of their empire!

In 1897 an expedition set off to chat to him about this. It was made up of a group of British traders, 250 native bearers to carry their luggage … and a drum and pipe band! They set off on 2 January. On 12 January *The Times* newspaper reported bad news:

> **The Times**
> **12 January 1897**
>
> ## EXPEDITION TRAGEDY
>
> Alarming news has reached London from the West Coast of Africa. A party of British men has been captured, and possibly murdered, near Benin City.

The British police chief in West Africa was Captain Alan Boisragon. A few weeks after the newspaper report he sent a telegram to his wife. It was a one-word telegram which said...

> **Telegram**
>
> Saved!
>
> from Sapelle, West Africa, to Mrs Alan Boisragon

Mrs Boisragon was probably pleased to hear that! But imagine if he'd had time to describe all the gory details in a letter! A letter like this...

115

My dearest wife,

Saved! It was a miracle. As you know we set off to meet Oba Overami in Benin City on 2 January. After taking a steamer and smaller boats up Gwato Creek we landed to walk the last 25 miles. All along the road we were met by friendly people with warm greetings from their king, Oba Overami.

Our revolvers were mostly locked in the luggage cases because we were expecting no trouble. By 5 January we were about halfway there when we came across a fallen tree. Behind the tree was an army of Oba Overami's men armed with muskets and hatchets. They opened fire and began a horrific massacre. As soon as our men fell they had their heads hacked off.

Robert Locke was lucky. He'd stopped to tie his bootlace and was at the back of our group. I was wounded and staggered into the thick forest where I came across Locke. We were the only two British survivors. I have heard that Kenneth Campbell was captured alive but Oba Overami had him taken to a nearby village and beheaded.

Locke and I wandered through the swamps and bush with only dew to drink and leaves to eat. Locke had a revolver and killed several natives who followed us. I was wounded again as I tried to beat them off with a stick. It was five days before we reached a friendly Beni village and then we were brought back to the British stronghold at Sapelle. They say we picked a bad time to visit Benin City. Oba Overami was slaughtering slaves that week and didn't want to be disturbed! How were we to know?

When I am fit to travel I will return home, my love. But you have not heard the last of Benin. The British Empire will not stand for this, you'll see. We will return, and next time we will have our trusty Maxim guns.

Your loving husband,

Alan

All the horrible facts in the letter are true.

Rawson's revenge

Sir Harry Rawson was given the job of leading the war of revenge. His troops marched through temperatures as high as 130° (Fahrenheit) – but there were horrors more sick-making than heat.

Alan Boisragon reported…

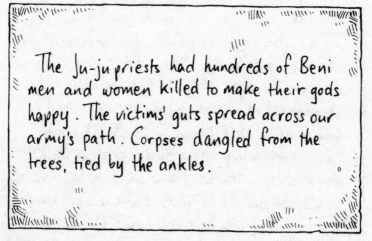

The Ju-ju priests had hundreds of Beni men and women killed to make their gods happy. The victims' guts spread across our army's path. Corpses dangled from the trees, tied by the ankles.

(This did NOT stop the enemy … so don't try it if you are being hunted down by the school bully! Try scattering banana skins instead!)

Rawson's army entered Benin City but Oba and the Ju-ju men had fled – leaving behind a town that 'smelled of human blood' (a reporter said). The Brits also found…

- two victims, crucified.
- deep holes filled with corpses.
- a field covered in a carpet of human bones.
- wells full of bodies – including one of Alan Boisragon's servants – amazingly still alive!

- Ju-ju temples with the remains of human sacrifices.

These were the horrors that Oba Overami had tried to stop Alan Boisragon's expedition from seeing. In the end the Maxim guns destroyed every Benin army it met. Oba Overami was captured and told to kneel down and eat the soil at his feet. The new British ruler said...

> *Now this is white man's country. There is only one king in this country, and that is the white man.*

Oba Overami had lost his kingdom and the Brits had added another piece of land to their empire.

DISGUSTOMETER RATING:

Suffering Sri Lanka

- The island of Sri Lanka was full of rich temples and peaceful people – the Singhalese – until the Portuguese arrived and started pinching their gold and their spices and their jewels and their women. The peaceful people fought back.

- They didn't have European guns but they were great at hiding in forests and setting traps and ambushes. Guns are great killers – but they're not much use when a Singhalese team drops a boulder on your head as you walk under a cliff!

SUCCESSFUL SINGHALESE

SOLDIER SAUSAGE

- And, if they captured you, they could teach you a lesson you'd never forget. Fifty Portuguese prisoners were sent back to their camp with TEN eyes between them – and they'd all had their naughty bits cut off too! Ouch!

When the Brits arrived in 1795 the Singhalese had some nasty tricks up their sleeves. Because of their Buddhist religion they were not so keen on taking the life of their Brit enemies so what did they do?

a) Left them out in the rain to catch cold and die.

b) Gave them food that was a week old so they'd get food poisoning and die.

c) Laid them on the ground and got a trained elephant to trample on them.

OH, IT'S A HORRIBLE JOB. YOU'LL BE PICKING BITS OF SQUISHED BRIT FROM BETWEEN YOUR TOES FOR WEEKS!

Answer:
c) It could have been worse. They could have been made to suffer those awful elephant jokes and been bored to death. You know the sort of thing. What do you get if you cross an elephant with a whale? A huge pair of swimming trunks. (*Yawn!*) What do you get if you cross an elephant with a butterfly? A mam–moth. (*Yawn! Yawn!*) What's the difference between an elephant and a banana? Have you tried peeling an elephant? (*Hey! That's not so bad!*)

The British army tried to attack the Singhalese king in his mountain palace but were forced to make peace. The Singhalese said the Brits were free to go back to their camp on the coast ... and they could leave the 149 wounded Brits in the hospital. The Singhalese promised to take care of them. They took care of them all right! Of the 149, only two lived to tell the bloody tale. One survivor, Sergeant Theon, reported...

> They mostly knocked out our soldiers' brains with clubs, then pulled the dead and dying out by the heels. They threw many down a well and many bodies were left in the streets to be eaten by dogs. But none were buried.

Sergeant Theon woke under a pile of bodies. A guard saw him and hanged him ... but the rope broke and he crawled away to hide in a hut. A week later he was captured again and this time he was treated well. He then married a Singhalese woman and stayed on the island. He clearly enjoyed hanging around the place!

IF YOU CAN'T KILL ME, MARRY ME!

The army that had left him behind weren't so lucky, though. The Singhalese changed their minds and attacked the Brits before they reached the coast. Every soldier was beheaded ... except for Corporal George Barnsley. His executioner chopped his neck and Barnsley fell. He was amazed to find he was still alive, so he pretended to be dead and later escaped.

Barnsley was a Brit hero – but a drunk. (He was lucky to have a neck to pour the booze down!) He was sent home to Britain and drank himself to death two years later.

DISGUSTOMETER RATING:

The awful Ashanti

The Ashanti tribe of West Africa were slave traders and head-hunters. Each warrior carried a knife to lop off the head of a dead enemy. Were the Brits worried by this? No, because the Ashanti lands were rich in ivory, gold and slaves, and the greedy, grasping Brits wanted a share, as usual.

They did good business with the Ashanti – till Britain banned slavery in the Empire. Then Brit Governor Sir Charles McCarthy tried to stop the Ashanti slavers so they cut off his head. But he was a brave enemy, so they did him a great honour ... they turned his skull into a drinking cup for great royal events!

One of the nastiest Ashanti tricks was to cut telegraph wires so the Brit forts were cut off from the cities, and the Brits had to use messengers to carry letters. The Ashanti would then...

- capture the Brit messengers
- hang them up by the ankles
- use the cut telegraph wire to whip their feet till they bled.

The messengers were then set free to carry the messages ... if they could!

But the Ashanti had one curious custom the Brits failed to stop. The worship of *stools*! The Ashanti believed that the ghosts of their dead friends lived inside the wooden stools of the tribal chiefs. These stools were the holiest things in the land. But one stool, held by the Ashanti king, was the holiest stool of all. It was a golden stool and was buried, they said, at the king's palace. There was one golden rule about the golden stool:

NO ONE SITS ON THE STOOL!

It may have LOOKED like a stool but it wasn't for sitting on. Think of a Christian church today. It has an altar that LOOKS like a table but you don't sit and eat your baked beans off it! But Brit Governor Fred Hodgson was too stupid and big-headed to understand this. In March 1900 he marched into the Ashanti capital and demanded the stool.

YOUR KING IS CAPTURED. SO IN FUTURE YOUR LEADER IS MIGHTY EMPRESS QUEEN VICTORIA!

FAIR ENOUGH

AS YOUR NEW LEADER, QUEEN VICTORIA MUST HAVE THAT STOOL

SHE SHOULD REALLY

And a bloody war started all because Hopeless Hodgson wanted to sit on a stool. Over a thousand Brits and countless Ashanti died. The Brits won through in the end, but that holy golden stool was never found and Queen Vic never got her fat bot on it. So was it all worth it?

DISGUSTOMETER RATING:

Did you know…?

Using someone's skull as a drinking cup is disgusting. But don't think that it was only the Ashanti who had such horribly historical ideas!

In 1884 the nutty General Gordon went to Khartoum (Sudan) to help the British soldiers trapped there. Goofy Gordon decided to stay and got himself massacred by the enemy 'dervishes' – which probably served him right.

Gordon was followed by General Kitchener, who defeated the dervishes then ordered that the dead dervish leader should have his grave wrecked. He took the skull and had it made into a desktop decoration to hold ink-pots and pens!

A leader of his people (and Kitchener)

Queen Victoria was shocked, so he gave up the idea. But kruel Kitchener was a Brit national hero for the next 30 years!

Epilogue

Britain has always been a tiny group of islands … tiny in size, that is, though their effect on the rest of the world has been enormous. Britain created an empire which changed the world – and made herself very rich in the process. The trouble is, 'great' deeds like that cost a lot – they cost a lot of pain and suffering. The native peoples that the Brits met were conquered, broken and sometimes even wiped out.

If you had stopped a British conqueror and asked, 'Why are you doing this?' he (or she) might have said…

If you'd asked them 'How are you doing this?' then honest empire-builders would have had to answer…

Most Victorian people believed their country was the…

LAND OF HOPE AND GLORY… MOTHER OF THE FREE!

The terrible truth is that the only 'free' ones were the white natives of the British Isles (and even then life was usually miserable unless you were wealthy).

The British Empire did help to get rid of a lot of evils, like cannibalism and human sacrifice – but it taught the conquered natives some new evils instead, like how to love money and how to massacre with machines.

Throughout the twentieth century, especially after the Second World War, the native peoples were slowly given back the lands that belonged to them. Some fought and died for that freedom – some were handed it by the Brits, who started to see how the world had changed. Empires were no longer a grand and glorious thing to have – just a sign of a greedy grasping nation and an excuse to be a bully. Since the Second World War, and Mr Hitler's attempts to build an evil empire, no one puts up with bullies any more.

The British Empire is now dead but no one can quite agree on just how good – or bad – it was. Some Brits say…

THE BRITISH EMPIRE ABOLISHED SLAVERY!

But you could remind them…

Maybe you should ask the people who had to put up with it how much good the British Empire did them! On 15 August 1947 the Brits gave back India, Pakistan and Bangladesh to the native people. The British politician Winston Churchill said...

The Indian Empire was the finest achievement of the British people!

What did the Indians think? They celebrated 15 August 1947 and freedom by tearing down the statues of the British Generals and the British rulers that the Brits had erected over the past 200 years.

So was the British rule of India a good thing for India and for the world?

Depends on who you ask!

BARMY
BRITISH EMPIRE

GRISLY QUIZ

Now find out if you're a
barmy British Empire expert!

BOLD BRITISH EMPIRE QUIZ

You've probably gathered that the Brits were a selfish bunch – they wanted the world and they stopped at nothing to get it. Take this quick quiz and see how well you know those evil empire-builders.

1. Why did early empire-builders take to the seas?
a) They wanted to get rich through trade with other countries
b) They wanted to learn the ways of other people
c) They wanted to find out if the Earth was really flat

2. What was the free-for-all sale of slaves known as?
a) A scrabble
b) A "Buy one get one free"
c) A scramble

3. What happened when the slave trade ended in Britain?
a) The freed slaves were given their own country
b) The freed slaves threw a great party with fireworks and cake
c) There was a riot in which loads of slave owners were killed

4. What was a bastinado?
a) A basket used by slaves to carry cotton
b) A form of punishment for slaves who didn't do as they were told
c) A prison for bad slaves

5. How were Indian rebels punished?
a) They were made to eat pig fat
b) They were forced to eat a really hot curry
c) They were made to lick up the blood from the people who had been killed

6. How were the native Aborigines of Tasmania treated by the posh governors of the prison colonies?
a) They were taken in and fed cucumber sandwiches
b) They were hunted for sport like animals
c) They were kept in cages and people paid to come and see them

7. What did the Barmy Brits give the Maoris in exchange for New Zealand?
a) Alcohol and guns
b) The island of Tasmania
c) A good beating

8. What did Shaka the Zulu do to his soldiers who forgot to bring their spears to their stabbing lessons?
a) He made them write 'I must not forget my spear' 100 times in the sand
b) He made them practise with a stick
c) He had them killed

Quick Questions

When the Beastly Brits arrived in their new territories they often set about killing the locals and generally being cruel conquerors. See if you can answer these questions about the Brits and their beastly behaviour.

1. Queen Victoria ruled over the great British Empire. She was Queen of Great Britain and Ireland, but she also had another title. What was it? (Clue: She certainly made an Empression)

2. Where did the Brits decide to send their convicts so they could keep their own country criminally clear? (Clue: Surely it's Oz-ious?)

3. What was the name of the drug that the British and the Chinese went to war over in the nineteenth century? (Clue: I 'ope you remember the answer to this!)

4. How were slaves punished by their mean masters if they tried to run away? (Clue: Has this question got you beaten?)

5. How did the Brits finally defeat the Maoris of New Zealand? (Clue: Pray don't attack on this day.)

6. How did horrible Henry Stanley punish slaves who rebelled in the Congo? (Clue: It's a handy way of cutting out the trouble)

7. What did the Zulus use as shields when facing the British spears? (Clue: There's no friend like a dead friend)

8. What did the name of the nasty Indian rebel group Thugees mean? (Clue: It has a hidden meaning)

THE SICKENING SLAVE TRADE

The 1700s were a sorry time for slaves. Caught and savagely shipped to foreign shores, they were forced to live a life of peril and punishment. But which of these sad slave stories are true and which are false?

1. African slaves were often captured by members of other African tribes and sold to traders.

2. Criminals were never sold to slave dealers as they were put to work by their own tribes.

3. Slaves were worth a lot of money, so they were well-treated on the voyage.

4. Britain was the smallest slave-trading nation in Europe, so it shouldn't be judged too harshly.

5. Many British people believed that keeping slaves was a kindness and that freeing them would be cruel.

6. One in five of the captured slaves died within the first four years of life on the plantations.

7. When slavery ended, the plantation owners were given money to make up for their lost workers (or the fact that they had to start paying them something!)

8. After they were freed, some plantation slaves earned so much money that they bought the plantations.

HORRIBLE HEROES

Many men became famous – or infamous – for their evil actions and cool crusades. Can you match the man (or woman!) with their mission?

1. Henry Morton Stanley
2. T. E. Lawrence
3. Harry Rawson
4. David Livingstone
5. Florence Nightingale
6. Robert Clive
7. Captain James Cook
8. Robert Baden-Powell

a) Went to Africa to stop the slave trade
b) Went to the Crimea to cure sick soldiers
c) Went to India to take advantage of trade
d) Went to Africa to overcome the Ottomans
e) Went to South Africa to butcher the Boers
f) Went to Africa to conquer the Congo
g) Took to the seas to take new territory
h) Went to Benin to kill the king

Bold British Empire Quiz
1a) 2c) 3a) 4b) 5c) 6b) 7a) 8c)

Quick Questions
1. Empress of India
2. Australia
3. Opium
4. They were flogged (whipped)
5. They attacked on a Sunday – a day of rest for the Maori's.
6. They had their hands cut off
7. The bodies of their comrades who had already been killed
8. It literally meant 'hidden'!

The Sickening Slave Trade
1. True. It wasn't just the slave traders who indulged in cruel kidnapping.
2. False. Criminals were among the first to be thrown to the dastardly slave dealers.
3. False. Nothing could be further from the truth – they were chained and packed in the hold like battery hens.
4. False. Not on your nelly! It might have been a small country, but Britain was the biggest slave-trading nation in Europe.
5. True. Barmy as it sounds, loads of peculiar people thought the slaves were better off in England than back in sunny Africa.
6. False. One in five? They should be so lucky! Half of them died in the first four years.

7. True. And the freed slaves got nothing!
8. False. They were paid so little that there were many rebellions.

Horrible Heroes
1f) 2d) 3h) 4a) 5b) 6c) 7g) 8e)

INTERESTING INDEX

Where will you find 'bad guts',
'eating ants' and 'smashed seals' in an index? In
a Horrible Histories book, of course!

Abolitionists (anti-slavery group) 8, 31, 34
Aborigines (Native Australians) 53–61
Albert (Victoria's husband/prince consort) 46, 49
ants, eating 84
Ashanti (West African tribe) 122–4

bad guts 104
Baden-Powell, Robert (British Boy Scout founder) 69, 74
Baker, Valentine (British soldier) 15
bastinado (painful punishment) 38–9
Beckford, William (British slave-trader) 24
beggars 14–15
boars 74–9
Boers (Dutch farmers in South Africa) 7, 9–10, 102
Boisragon, Alan (British police chief in Africa) 115–19
Bosman, William (British slave-trader) 26
Boswell, James (Scottish writer) 31–3
branding 26
bravery, when suffering 15, 40, 47, 51, 88–94
British navy 42

Bruce, James (British explorer) 8
bushrangers (British super-convicts in Tasmania) 55–6

cannibals 64–5
chains 29, 34, 80
    for elephants 68–9
    keeping slaves in 56
children 20, 59, 111
    as convicts 53–4
    falling into lavatory bucket 23
    massacred 45, 51–2
    working hard 27
cholera (dreadful disease) 50
Clive, Robert (leader of the British East India Co) 48
convicts 8–9, 53–6
Cook, James (British sea captain) 8
cows/cattle 44–5, 113
    replacing kangaroos 59
    shields made of 105
criminals, sold as slaves 21
crocodiles 48, 51, 74

Dervishes (Sudanese) 15
diamonds 18
Dingaan (Zulu leader) 101–4
dogs, deadly for 71–3, 78, 121
Doyle, Francis Hastings (British poet) 88–91
drink, dying from 51, 60, 91, 122
dysentery (dreadful disease) 24

East India Company (powerful trading company) 8
elephants, evil for 48, 52, 66–9, 82, 120
Equiano, Olaudah (African slave) 8, 20, 25
Eyre, Edward (British governor of Jamaica) 37, 39–40

food, foul 23–4, 94
Frobisher, Martin (British explorer) 11–12

games, gruesome 74–9
Gladstone, William (British prime minister) 10
goats 96, 98, 113
gold 9, 18, 24, 119, 122–3
Gordon, Charles (British general) 124
Gordon, G.W. (Jamaican priest) 40

Handland, Dorothy (British convict) 54
hands, chopping off 85
hanging 37–40, 48, 98, 111, 114,
heroes 80–94, 122
hippos 69–70, 81
historians, horrible 27, 45
Hodgson, Fred (British governor) 123–4
hog-hunting 74–6
holy golden stool 123–4
home-sickness, dying of 59
Hone Heke Pokai (Maori chief) 62–5
horses 74–7, 79, 88
Hudson, John (British chimney sweep/convict) 54

hyenas 76

Indian Mutiny 10, 43–5, 48, 50
Indians 8, 10, 14, 42–5, 47, 91, 95, 127
Inuit (Eskimos) 12
ivory 82, 122

King Billy (last Tasmanian native man) 60
Kitchener, Horatio Herbert (British general) 124
Knibb, William (British priest) 33

Leopold (king of Belgium) 80–1, 87
Livingstone, David (Scottish missionary) 9, 80–1, 88
L'Ouverture, Toussant (slave rebel leader) 8

machine-guns 84, 105, 112–13, 117, 119
Maoris (Native New Zealanders) 10, 61–5
Marmon, Jackey (British ex-convict in New Zealand) 64–5
Maxim gun (machine-gun) 112–13, 117, 119
money-making 15–19, 23, 34, 127
musical instruments, making 27–8
mutiny, caused by cartridges 43–4

Napier, Charles (British general) 91–2
Native Americans 11
natives 12–14, 38, 54–65, 82–7, 92, 95–124
New Zealanders 61–5
Newton, John (British captain) 22
Nicholson, John (British soldier/god) 47, 49

Oba Overami (king of Benin) 114, 116–19
Opium Wars 9, 108–12
overseers (slave managers) 27, 38, 80

pigs 44, 74, 79
  bladders 28

sewn into skins of 45
Pilgrim Fathers (British colonists in America) 7
Popham, Hope (British admiral) 92–3
punishments, painful 32–3, 37–41, 45, 51, 68–9, 106
Purchas, Simon (British puritan) 11
Puritans (Christians) 11
pygmies 87

Rawson, Harry (British soldier) 118
rebellions 29–31, 36–7, 48, 84–5
recipes, revolting 78–9
revenge 64–5
Rose, Hugh (British governor of Beirut) 38
rubber 80, 84–5

salt, rubbed in wounds 41
scrambles (slave sales) 25
seals, smashed 93
sepoys (Indian soldiers) 43–5
Shaka (Zulu chief) 9, 104–8
Sjoblom, E.V. (Swedish missionary) 85
skulls
    as a drinking cup 122
    necklaces of 97
    paths of 114
slavery 7–9, 18–42, 55–6, 80, 87, 114, 117, 127
Sleeman, William (British colonel) 98
songs, sad 27, 38
sports, sick 74–9, 99–101
Sri Lankans 119–22
Stanley, Henry Morton (British explorer) 80–8
strangling season 97
sunstroke, dying from 14
superstitions, strange 35

Tacky's Revolt (Jamaican slave rebellion) 40
Tasmanians 54–60
tattoos, on eyelids 98

Thuggees (Indian killer cult) 46, 49, 95–8
tigers, superstitions about 108–9
Tipu (Indian prince) 42–3
trade, treacherous 16–19, 38
tricks, terrible 61, 85–6, 122
Truganini (last Tasmanian woman) 60
tusks, uses for 66–7

Victoria (British queen/empress) 9–10, 36, 46–9, 61–3, 72, 87, 123–4
Victoria Cross 72

whips 27, 34, 38, 80–1, 93–4, 122

Zulus (southern African tribe) 9–10, 79, 91, 101–8

Terry Deary was born at a very early age, so long ago he can't remember. But his mother, who was there at the time, says he was born in Sunderland, north-east England, in 1946 – so it's not true that he writes all *Horrible Histories* from memory. At school he was a horrible child only interested in playing football and giving teachers a hard time. His history lessons were so boring and so badly taught, that he learned to loathe the subject. *Horrible Histories* is his revenge.

Martin Brown was born in Melbourne, on the proper side of the world. Ever since he can remember he's been drawing. His dad used to bring back huge sheets of paper from work and Martin would fill them with doodles and little figures. Then, quite suddenly, with food and water, he grew up, moved to the UK and found work doing what he's always wanted to do: drawing doodles and little figures.